The

Impersonal Life

Joseph S. Benner

Contents

Foreword

We cannot alter external things, nor shape other people to our liking, nor mould the world to our wishes but we can alter internal things, — our desires, passions, thoughts, — we can shape our liking to other people, and we can mould the inner world of our own mind in accordance with wisdom, and so reconcile it to the outer world if men and things. The turmoil of the world we cannot avoid, but the disturbances of mind we can overcome. The duties and difficulties of life claim our attention, but we can rise above all anxiety concerning them. Surrounded by noise, we can yet have a quiet mind; involved in responsibilities, the heart can be at rest; in the midst of strife, we can know the abiding peace. The eighteen pieces which comprise this book, unrelated as some of them are in the letter, will be found to be harmonious in the spirit, in that they point the reader towards those heights of self-knowledge and self-conquest which, rising above the turbulance of the world, lift their peaks where the Heavenly Silence reigns.

James Allen

1

I Am

To you who read, I speak.

To you, who, through long years and much running to and fro, have been eagerly seeking, in books and teachings, in philosophy and religion, for you know not what Truth, Happiness, Freedom, God;

To you whose Soul is weary and discouraged and almost destitute of hope;

To you, who many times have obtained a glimpse of that "Truth" only to find, when you followed and tried to reach it, that it disappeared in the beyond, and was but the mirage of the desert;

To you, who thought you had found it in some great teacher, who was perhaps the acknowledged head of some Society, Fraternity or Religion, and who appeared to you to be a "Master," so marvelous was the wisdom he taught and the works he performed; only to awaken later to the realization that that "Master" was but a human personality, with faults and weaknesses, and secret sins, the same as you, even though that personality may have been a channel through which were voiced many beautiful teachings, which seemed to you the highest "Truth;"

And here you are, Soul aweary and enhungered, and not knowing where to turn—

To you, I AM come.

Likewise to you, who have begun to feel the presence of that "Truth" within your Soul, and seek the confirmation of that which of late has been vaguely struggling for living expression within.

Yes, to all you who hunger for the true "Bread of Life," I AM come.

Are you ready to partake?

If so, then arouse yourself. Sit up. Still your human mind and follow closely My Word herein spoken.

Or you will turn away disappointed once more, with the aching hunger still in your heart.

I!

Who am I?—

I, Who speak with such seeming knowledge and authority?

Listen!

I AM You, that part of you who IS and KNOWS; WHO KNOWS ALL THINGS,

And always knew, and always was.

Yes, I AM You, Your SELF; that part of you who says I AM and is I AM;

That transcendent, innermost part of you which quickens within as you read, which responds to this My Word, which perceives Its Truth, which recognizes all Truth and discards all error wherever found. Not that part which has been feeding on error all these years.

For I AM your real Teacher, the only real one you will ever know, and the only MASTER;

I, your Divine SELF.

I, the I AM of you, bring to you this My Message, My living Word, as I have brought to you everything in life, be it book or "Master" to teach you that I and I alone, your own True Self, AM The Teacher for you, the only Teacher and the only God, Who is and always has been providing you not only with the Bread and Wine of Life, but with all things needed for your physical, mental and spiritual growth and sustenance.

Therefore that which appeals to YOU, as you read, is MY Message, spoken to your outer human consciousness from within, and is but a confirmation of that which the I AM of you always knew within, but had not yet translated in definite, tangible terms to your outer consciousness.

Likewise, all that ever appealed to You, coming from some outward expression, was but the confirmation of My Word already spoken within. The outward expression was the avenue or means I chose at the time through which to reach and impress your human or self consciousness.

I AM not your human mind, nor its child, the intellect. They are but the expression of your Being, as you are the expression of My Being; they are but phases of your human personality, as You are a phase of My Divine Impersonality.

Weigh and study carefully these words.

Rise up and free yourself now and for always from the domination of your personality, with its self-inflated and self-glorifying mind and intellect.

For your mind henceforth must be Your servant, and the intellect Your slave, if My Word is to penetrate to your Soul consciousness.

I AM come now to your Soul consciousness, which I have quickened expressly in preparation for the reception of My Word.

Now, if you are strong enough to bear it;

If you can put aside all your private personal fancies, beliefs and opinions, which are but the rubbish you have gathered from the dumping grounds of others;

If you are strong enough to cast them all away;

Then My Word will be to you a source of endless Joy and Blessing. Be prepared to have this personality of yours doubt My Word as you read It all along the way;

For its very life is threatened, and it knows it cannot live and thrive and longer dominate your thinking, your feelings, your going and coming, as of old, if you take My Word into your heart and permit It there to abide. Yes, I AM come to you now,

To make you conscious of My Presence;

For I have likewise prepared your human mind so that it can, in a measure, comprehend the meaning of Me. I have been with you always, but you did not know it.

I have purposely led you through the Wilderness of books and teaching, of religions and philosophies, keeping ever before your Soul's eye the vision of the Promised Land; feeding you with the manna of the Desert, that you might remember and value and long for the Bread of the Spirit.

Now I have brought you to the river Jordan that separates you from your Divine heritage. Now the time has come for you consciously to know Me; the time has come for you to cross over into Canaan, the land of Milk and Honey.

Are you ready?

Do you want to go?

Then follow this My Word, which is the Ark of My Covenant, and you shall go over dry shod.

2

Be Still! *and* Know I Am God

Now, in order that you may learn to know Me, so that you can be *sure* it is I, you own True Self, Who speak these words, you must first learn to Be Still, to quiet your human mind and body and all their activities, so that you no longer are conscious of them.

You may not yet be able to do this, but I will teach you how, if you really want to know Me, and are willing to prove it by trusting Me and obeying Me in all that I now shall call upon you to do.

Listen!

Try to imagine the "I" who speaks throughout these pages as being your Higher or Divine Self, addressing and counseling your human mind and intellect, which you will consider for the moment as being a separate personality. Your human mind is so constituted that it cannot accept anything which does not conform with what it has previously experienced or learned, and which its intellect does not consider reasonable. Therefore, in addressing it, You are using such terms and expressions as will most clearly explain to your intellect the truths it must understand before the mind can awaken to the consciousness of your meaning.

The fact is, this "I" is yourself, your Real Self. Your human mind has heretofore been so engrossed with the task of supplying its intellect and body with all manner of selfish indulgences, that it has never had time to get acquainted with the Real You, its true Lord and Master. You have been so interested in and affected by the pleasures and sufferings of your body and intellect, that you have almost come to believe You are your intellect and body, and you have consequently nearly forgotten Me, your Divine Self.

I AM not your intellect and body, and this Message is to teach that You and I are One. The words I herein speak, and the main burden of these instructions, is to awaken your consciousness to this great fact.

You cannot awaken to this fact until you can get away from the consciousness of this body and intellect, which so long have held you enslaved. You must feel Me within, before you can know I AM there.

Now, in order that you can become wholly oblivious of your mind and its thoughts and your body and its sensations, so that you can feel Me within, it is necessary that you studiously obey these, My instructions.

Sit quietly in a relaxed position, and, when wholly at ease, let your mind take in the significance of these words:

"Be *still!* And KNOW – I AM God."

Without thinking, allow this, *My Divine Command,* to penetrate deep into your Soul. Let whatever impressions that come to your mind enter at will without effort or interference on your part. Note carefully their import, for it is I, within, through these impressions, instructing you. Then, when somewhat of their vital significance begins to dawn upon your consciousness, speak these My Words slowly, imperatively, to every cell of your body, to every faculty of your mind, with all the conscious power you possess: "

Be *still!* - and KNOW- I AM God."

Speak them just as they are herein written, trying to realize that the God of you commands and demands of your mortal self implicit obedience.

Study them, search out their hidden potency.

Brood over them, carry them with you into your work, whatever it be. Make them the vital, dominating factor in your work, in all your creative thoughts.

Say them a thousand times a day, Until you have discovered all My innermost meaning;

Until every cell of your body thrills in joyful response to the command, "Be Still," and instantly obeys;

And every vagrant thought hovering around your mind hides itself off into nothingness.

Then, as the Words reverberate through the caverns of your now empty being;

Then, as the Sun of Knowing begins to rise on the horizon of your consciousness; Then, will you feel the swell of a wondrous strange Breath filling you to the extreme of all your mortal members, causing your senses almost to burst with the ecstasy of it; then, will there come surge after surge of a mighty, resistless Power rising within you, lifting you almost off the earth; then, will you feel within the Glory, the Holiness, the Majesty of My Presence;

And then, *then* you will KNOW, I AM, God.

You, — when you have felt Me thus in such moments within, when you have tasted of My Power, hearkened to My Wisdom, and know the ecstasy of My all-embracing Love, no disease can touch, no circumstance can weaken, no enemy can conquer you. For now you KNOW I AM *within*, and you always hereafter will turn to Me in your need, putting all your trust in Me, and allowing Me to manifest My Will.

You, when you turn thus to Me, will always find Me an unfailing and ever-present help in time of need; for I will so fill you with a Realization of My Presence and of My Power, that you need only Be Still and allow Me to do whatever you want done — heal your ills and those of others, illumine your mind so you can see with My eyes the Truth you seek, or perform perfectly the tasks which before seemed almost impossible of accomplishment.

This Knowledge, this Realization, will not come at once. It may not come for years. It may come tomorrow.

It depends upon no one but *You*;

Not upon your personality, with its human desires and human understanding;

But upon the I AM of you —God, within.

Who is it that causes the bud to open into the blossom?

Who causes the chick to burst its shell?

Who decides the day and the hour?

It is the conscious, natural act of the Intelligence within, My Intelligence, directed by My Will, bringing to fruition My Idea and expressing it in the blossom and in the chick.

But did the blossom and the chick have anything to do with it?

No, only as they submitted or united their will with Mine and allowed Me and My Wisdom to determine the hour and the ripeness for action, and then only as they obeyed the impulse of My Will to make the effort, could they step forth into the New Life.

You may, with your personality, try a thousand times a thousand times to burst through the shell of your human consciousness.

It will result only, if at all, in a breaking down of the doors I have provided between the world of tangible forms and the real of intangible dreams; and the door being open, you then no longer can keep out intruders from your private domain, without much trouble and suffering.

But even through such suffering you may gain the strength you lack and the wisdom needed to know that, not until you yield up all desire for knowledge, for goodness, yes, for union with Me, to *benefit self*, can you unfold your petals showing forth the perfect Beauty of My Divine Nature, and throw off the shell of your human personality and step forth into the glorious Light of My Heavenly Kingdom.

Therefore I give you these directions now, at the beginning, that you may be learning how to recognize Me.

For I here promise you, if you follow and strive earnestly to comprehend and obey My instructions herein given, you shall very soon know Me, and I will give you to comprehend all of My Word wherever written, in book or teaching, in Nature, or in your fellow man.

If there is much in what herein is written that seems contradictory, seek out My real meaning before discarding it.

Do not leave a single paragraph, or any one thought in it, until all that is suggested becomes clear.

But in all your seeking and all your striving, let it be with faith and trust in Me, your True Self within, and without being anxious about results; for the results are all in My keeping, and I will take care of them. Your doubts and your anxiety are but of the personality, and if allowed to persist will lead only to failure and disappointment.

3

I, Life, God

If that which you have read has awakened a response within, and the Soul of you yearns for more, then you are ready for what follows.

If you still question or rebel at the seeming assumption of Divine authority for what is herein written, your intellect telling you it is but another attempt to beguile your mind with cunning suggestion and subtle sophistry, then you will receive no benefit from these words; for their meaning is as yet hidden from your mortal consciousness, and My Word must come to you through other avenues of expression.

It is well if your personality with its intellect impels you thus to question and rebel against authority you do not yet *know* to be Mine. It is really I Who cause your personality thus to rebel; for your personality with its proud sense of individuality is still needed by Me to develop a mind and body strong enough that they can perfectly express Me. Until you have become prepared to know Me it is but natural for your personality thus to question and rebel. Once you recognize My Authority, that moment the undermining of the authority of the personality has begun. The days of its dominion are numbered, and you will more and more turn to Me for help and guidance.

Therefore, be not dismayed. Read on, and mayhap the recognition will come. But know that you can read or not, as you choose; but if you do it is really I Who choose, and not you.

For you, who seemingly choose not to read further, I have plans, and in due season you shall learn that whatever you do, or like, or desire, it is I leading you through all the fallacies and illusions of the personality, that you may finally awaken to their unreality and then turn to Me as the one and only Reality. Then these words will find a response within: —

"Be still! — and KNOW— I AM God."

Yes, I AM that innermost part of you that sits within, and calmly waits and watches, knowing neither time nor space; for I AM the Eternal and fill all space.

I watch and wait for you to be done with your petty human follies and weaknesses, with your vain longings, ambitions and regrets, knowing that will come in time; and then you will turn to Me, weary, discouraged, empty and humble, and ask Me to take the lead, not realizing that I have been leading you all the time.

Yes, I sit here within, quietly waiting for this; yet while waiting it was really I Who directed all your ways, Who inspired all your thoughts and acts, impersonally utilizing and manipulating each so as eventually to bring you and My other human expressions to a final conscious recognition of Me.

Yes, I have been within always, deep within your heart. I have been with you through all, through your joys and heartaches, your successes and mistakes, through your evildoing, your shame, your crimes against your brother and against God, as you thought.

Aye, whether you went straight ahead, or strayed aside, or stepped backward, it was I Who brought you through.

It was I Who urged you on by the glimpse of Me in the dim distance. It was I Who lured you by a vision of Me in some bewitching face, or beautiful body, or intoxicating pleasure, or overpowering ambition.

It was I Who appeared before you within the garb of Sin, or Weakness, or Greed, or Sophistry, and drove you back into the arms of Conscience, leaving you to struggle in its shadowy grasp; until you awakened to its impotence, rose up in disgust, and in the inspiration of a new vision tore off My mask.

Yes, it is I Who causes you to do all things, and if you can see it, it is *I Who do all things that you do*, and all things that your brother does; for that in you and in him which IS, is I, My Self.

For I AM LIFE.

I AM the Innermost, the Spirit, the animating Cause of your being, of all life, of all living things, both visible and invisible. There is nothing dead, for I, the Impersonal ONE, AM all that there is. I AM Infinite and wholly unconfined; the Universe is My Body, all the Intelligence there is emanates from My Mind, all the Love there is flows from My Heart, all the Power there is, is but My Will in action.

The threefold Force, manifesting as all Wisdom, all Love, all Power, or if you will, as Light, Heat, and Energy — that which holds together all forms and is back of and in all expressions and phases of life, is but the manifestation of My Self in the act or state of Being.

Nothing can Be without manifesting and expressing some phase of Me, Who AM not only the Builder of all forms, but the Dweller in each. In the heart of each I dwell; in the heart of the human, in the heart of the animal, in the heart of the flower, in the heart of the stone. In the heart of each I live and move and have My Being, and from out the heart of each I send forth that phase of Me I desire to express, and which manifests in the outer world as a stone, a flower, an animal, a man.

Is there nothing, then, but this great *I*? Am I to be permitted no individuality for myself? I hear you ask.

No, there is nothing, absolutely nothing, that is not a part of Me, controlled and ruled eternally by Me, the *One* Infinite Reality.

As for your so-called individuality, that is nothing but your personality still seeking to maintain a separate existence.

Soon you shall know there is no individuality apart from My Individuality, and all personality shall fade away into My Divine Impersonality.

Yes, and you shall soon reach that state of awakening where you will get a glimpse of My Impersonality, and you will then desire no individuality, no separation for yourself; for you will see that is but one more illusion of the personality.

4

Consciousness, Intelligence, Will

Y es, I know the many mixed thoughts that have been crowding into your mind as you read, the doubts and eager questionings, the vague fear that imperceptibly changed into a growing hope that this glimmering of My Meaning, which has begun to penetrate the darkness of your human intellect, may shine brighter so you can see clearly the Truth which you instinctively feel is hidden beneath My Words.

Again I say, this I AM speaking herein is the Real Self of you, and in reading these words it is necessary that you realize it is You, your own Self, that is speaking them to your human consciousness, in order fully to comprehend their meaning.

I also repeat, this is the same I AM that is the Life and Spirit animating all living things in the Universe, from the tiniest atom to the greatest Sun; that this I AM is the Intelligence in you and in your brother and sister; and that it is likewise the Intelligence which causes everything to live and grow and become that which it is their destiny to be.

Perhaps you cannot yet understand how this I AM can be, at one and the same time, the I AM of you and the I AM of your brother, and also the Intelligence of the stone, the plant, and the animal.

You will see this, however, if you follow these My Words and obey the instructions herein given; for I will soon bring to your consciousness a Light that will illumine the deepest recesses of your mind and drive away all the clouds of human misconceptions, ideas and opinions that now darken your intellect, if you read on and strive earnestly to comprehend My Meaning.

So listen carefully.

I AM You, the Real Self of you, All that you *really* are. That which you think you are, you are *not*. That is only an illusion, a shadow of the *Real* You, which is I, your Immortal, Divine Self.

I AM that point of consciousness focalized in your human mind which calls itself "I". I AM that "I", but that which you call your consciousness is in reality *My* Consciousness, thinned down to suit the capacity of your human mind. It is still *My* Consciousness, and when you can drive from your mind all its human misconceptions, ideas and opinions, and can cleanse and empty it utterly, so that *My* Consciousness can have a chance to express freely, then you will recognize *Me* and you will know that you are nothing being only a focal center of My Consciousness, an avenue of medium through which I can express *My* meaning — in matter.

Perhaps you cannot see this yet, and of course cannot believe it until I fully prepare your mind by convincing your intellect of its truth.

You have been told that each cell of your body has a consciousness and an intelligence of its own; that were it not for this consciousness it could not do the work it so intelligently does.

Each cell is surrounded by millions of other cells, each intelligently doing its own work and each evidently controlled by the united consciousness of all these cells, forming a *group* intelligence, which directs and controls this work; this group intelligence apparently being the intelligence of the *organ* which the cells comprising it form.

Likewise, there are other group intelligences in other organs, each containing other millions of cells, and all these organs make up your physical body.

Now, you know *You* are the Intelligence that directs the work of the organs of your body, whether this directing is done consciously or unconsciously; and that each cell of each organ is really a focal center of this directing Intelligence; and that when this Intelligence is withdrawn the cells fall apart, your physical body dies and exists no more as a living organism.

Who is this *You* who directs and controls the activities of your organs, and consequently of each cell composing them?

You cannot say it is your human or personal self who does this, for you of yourself consciously can control the action of scarcely a single organ of your body.

It must then be this Impersonal I AM of you, which is You, and yet is not you.

Listen!

You, the I AM of you, are to Me what the cell consciousness of your body is to your I AM Consciousness.

You are a cell, as it were, of My Body, and your consciousness (as one of My Cells) is to Me what the consciousness of one of the cells of your body is to You.

Therefore, it must be that the consciousness of the cell of your body is My Consciousness, even as your consciousness is My Consciousness; and therefore We must be One in consciousness — the cell, You and I.

You cannot now consciously direct or control a single cell of your body; but when you can at will enter into the Consciousness of the I AM of you and know its identity with Me, *then you can control not only every cell of your body, but that of any other body you might wish to control.*

What happens when your consciousness no longer controls the cells of your body? The body disintegrates, the cells separate, and their work for the time being is finished. But do the cells die or lose consciousness? No, they simply sleep or rest for a period, and after a while unite with other cells and form new combinations, and sooner or later appear in other manifestations of life, perhaps mineral, perhaps vegetable, perhaps animal; showing that they still retain their original consciousness and but await the action of My Will to join together in a new organism to do the work of the new consciousness through which I desire to manifest.

Then apparently this cell consciousness is a consciousness common to all bodies, mineral, vegetable, animal, human, each cell fitted perhaps by experience for a certain general kind of work?

Yes, this cell consciousness is common to every cell of every body, no matter what its kind, because it is an Impersonal consciousness, having no purpose other than doing the work allotted it. It lives only to work wherever needed. When through with building one form, it takes up the work of building another, under whatever consciousness I desire it to serve.

Thus it is likewise with you.

You, as one of the cells of My Body, have a consciousness that is My Consciousness, an intelligence that is My Intelligence, even a will that is My Will. You have none of these for yourself or of yourself. They are all Mine and for My use only.

Now, My consciousness and My Intelligence and My Will are wholly Impersonal, and therefore are common with you and with all the cells of My Body, even as they are common with all the cells of your body.

I AM the directing Intelligence of All, the animating Spirit, the Life, the Consciousness of all matter, of all Substance. If you can see it, *You,* the *Real* you, the *Impersonal* you, are in all and are one with all, are in Me and are one with Me; just as I AM in you and in all, and thereby am expressing My Reality through you and through all.

This will, which you call your will, is likewise no more yours personally than is this consciousness and this intelligence of your mind and of the cells of your body yours.

It is but that small portion of My Will which I permit the personal you to use. Just as fast as you awaken to recognition of a certain power or faculty within you and begin consciously to use it, do I allow you that much more of My Infinite Power.

All power and its use is but so much recognition and understanding of the use of My Will. Your will and all your powers are only phases of My Will, which I supply to suit your capacity to use it.

Were I to entrust you with the full power of My Will, before you know how consciously to use it, it would annihilate your body utterly.

To test your strength and more often to show you what the misuse of My Power does to you, I at times allow you to commit a sin, so-called, or to make a mistake. I even permit you to become inflated with the sense of My Presence within you, when It manifests as a consciousness of My Power, My Intelligence, My Love; and I let you take these and use them for your own personal purposes. But not for long— for, not being strong enough to control them, they soon take the bit in their teeth, run away with you, throw you down in the mire, and disappear from your consciousness for the time being.

Always I AM there to pick you up, after the fall, although you do not know it at the time; first straightening you out and then starting you onward again, by pointing out the reason for your fall; and finally, when you are sufficiently humbled, causing you to see that these powers accruing to you by the conscious use of My Will, My Intelligence and My Love, are allowed you only for use in My Service, and not at all for your own personal ends.

Do the cells of your body, the muscles of your arm, think to set themselves up as having a separate will from your will, or a separate intelligence from your intelligence?

No, they know no intelligence but yours, no will but yours.

After a while it will be that you will realize you are only one of the cells of My Body; and that your will is not your will, but Mine; that what consciousness and what intelligence you have are Mine wholly; and that there is no such person as you, you personally being only a physical form containing a human brain, which I created for the purpose of expressing in matter and Idea, a certain phase of which I could express best only in that particular form.

All this may be difficult for you now to accept, and you may protest very strenuously that it cannot be, that every instinct of your nature rebels against such yielding and subordinating yourself to an unseen and unknown power, however Impersonal or Divine.

Fear not, it is only your personality that thus rebels. If you continue to follow and study My Words, all will soon be made clear, and I will surely open up to your inner understanding many wonderful Truths that now are impossible for you to comprehend. Your Soul will rejoice sing glad praises, and you will bless these words for the message they bring.

5

The Key

Now you may not even yet know I AM, or believe that I AM really you, or that I AM likewise your brother and your sister, and that you are all parts of Me and One with Me.

You may not realize that the Souls of you and your brother and sister, the only real and imperishable parts of the mortal you, are but different phases of Me in expression in what is called Nature.

Likewise you may not realize that you and your brothers and sisters are phases or attributes of My Divine Nature, just as your human personality, with its mortal body, mind and intellect, is a phase of your human nature.

No, you do not realize this yet, but I speak of it now, that you may know the signs when they begin to appear in your consciousness, as they surely will.

In order to recognize these signs, all that now follows must be considered carefully and studied, and should not be passed by until My meaning, at least in some degree, is grasped. Once you fully understand the principle I here set down, then all My Message will become clear and comprehensible.

I first give you the Key that will unlock every mystery that now hides from you the secret of My Being.

This Key, when you once know how to use it, will open the door to all Wisdom and all Power in heaven and earth. Yea, it will open the door to the Kingdom of Heaven, and then you have but to enter in to become consciously One with Me.

This Key is

"To THINK is to CREATE," or

"As you THINK in your HEART, so is it with you".

Stop and meditate on this that it may get firmly fixed in your mind.

A Thinker is a Creator.

A Thinker lives in a world of his own *conscious* creation.

When you once know *how* "to think," you can create at will anything you wish, whether it be a new personality, a new environment, or a new world.

Let us see if you cannot grasp some of the Truths hidden and controlled by this Key.

You have been shown how all consciousness is One, and how it is all *My* Consciousness, and yet is also yours and likewise that of the animal, the plant, the stone, and the invisible cell.

You have seen how this consciousness is controlled by My *Will*, which causes the invisible cells to unite and form the various organisms for the expression and use of the different Centers of Intelligence through which I desire to express.

But *you* cannot yet see how you can direct and control the consciousness of the cells of your own body, not to speak of those of other bodies, even if you and I and they are all one in consciousness and intelligence.

By paying special attention to what follows, however, you now may be enabled to see this. Have you ever taken the pains to study out what is consciousness? How it seems to be an impersonal state of awareness, of waiting to serve or to be directed or used by some power latent in and intimately related to itself?

How man seems to be merely the highest type of organism containing this consciousness, which is directed and used by this *power* within itself?

That this power latent in man's consciousness and in all consciousness is nothing but Will, My Will? For you know that all power is but the manifestation of My Will.

Now you have been told that in the beginning I created man in "My Image and Likeness," after which I breathed into him the Breath of Life and he became a Living Soul.

By creating man in My Image and Likeness I created an organism capable of expressing all of My Consciousness and all of My Will, which means likewise all of My *Power*, My *Intelligence*, and My *Love*. I therefore made it *perfect* in the beginning, patterning it after My own Perfection.

When I breathed into man's organism My Breath, it became alive with Me; for then it was I breathed into it My Will not from without, but from *within* from the Kingdom of Heaven *within*, where always I AM. Ever afterward I breathed and lived and had My Being *within* man, for I created him in My Image and Likeness only for that purpose.

The proof of this is, man does not and cannot breathe of himself. Something far greater than his conscious, natural self lives in his body and breathes through his lungs. A mighty power within his body thus uses the lungs, even as it uses the heart to force the blood containing the life it in-drew through the lungs to every cell of the body; as it uses the stomach and other organs to digest and assimilate food to make blood, tissue, hair and bone; as it uses the brain, the tongue, the hands and feet, to think and say and do everything that man does.

This power is My Will to BE and LIVE in man.

Therefore, whatever man is, I AM, and whatever man does, or you do, I do, and whatever you say or think, it is I Who say or think it through your organism.

You were also told that when man was thus possessed of My Breath he was given dominion over all the kingdoms of the earth. Which means he was made lord of the earth, the sea, the air and the ethers, and all beings living in all these kingdoms paid him homage and were subject to his will.

This naturally was so, for I, within man's consciousness and within all consciousness, AM always manifesting My Will; and I, the lord and ruler of man's organism, AM likewise the lord and ruler of all organisms in which consciousness dwells. As all consciousness is My Consciousness and It dwells wherever there is life, and as there is no substance in which there is not life, then My Consciousness must be in everything, in earth, water, air and fire, and therefore must fill all space. In fact it is space, or that which man calls space.

Then My Will, being the power latent in all consciousness, must reach everywhere.

Therefore man's will, which is but a focalization of My Will, must likewise reach everywhere; hence the consciousness of all organisms, including his own, is subject to man's direction and control.

All it needs is for him consciously to realize this, realize that I, the Impersonal Self within him, AM constantly directing, controlling and using the consciousness of all organisms every moment of every day of his life.

I AM doing this by and through his *thinking*.

I AM doing this with and through man's organism. Man thinks he thinks; but it is I, the Real I of him, who thinks through his organism. Through this *thinking and his spoken word* I accomplish all that man does, and make man and his world all that they are.

It makes no difference if man and his world are *not* what *he* supposes they are.

They are just what I created them to be for *My* Purpose.

But, if I do all the thinking, man does not and cannot think, I hear you say.

Yes, here seems a mystery, but it will be revealed to you, if you note carefully what follows:

For I AM going to teach you —man—*HOW* to think.

6

Thinking *and* Creating

I have said that man does not think; that it is I, within him, Who do his thinking.

I have also said man *thinks* he thinks.

As this is an apparent contradiction. I needs must show you that man ordinarily, does not think, any more than he does anything else he *supposes* he does.

For I, within him, do *all* that he does; but I necessarily do it through his organism, through his personality, his body, mind and soul. I will point out how this can be.

First, try to realize that I made you in My Image and Likeness, and that I have My Being within you. Even if you do not know this now and believe that I, God, AM somewhere without, and that we are separated, try for the time being to *imagine* I AM within you.

Next, realize that which you do when you think is not real thinking, because it is not conscious thinking; for you are unconscious of Me, the Inspirer and Director of every idea and thought that enters your mind. Next, realize because I AM within you, and you are My Image and Likeness, and therefore possess all of My Faculties, you have the power of thinking; but not being conscious that thinking is creating and that it is one of My Divine Powers you are using you have indeed all your life been thinking, but it has all been mis-thinking, or what you would call error-thinking.

And this error-thinking, this not knowing it is My Power you have been thus misusing, has been separating you in consciousness farther and farther from Me; but all the time fulfilling My Purpose, which later on will be made manifest to you.

The proof of this is, you *think* you are separated from Me, that you are living in a material World, that your body of Flesh engenders and harbors pleasure and pain, and that an evil influence, called the Devil, is manifesting in the world, opposing My Will.

Yes, you think all these things are so.

They are — to you, for all things are to man's mortal consciousness what he *thinks* or *believes* they are.

I have likewise caused them to appear to man to be what he thinks they are. This also is to suit My purpose, and to fulfill the law of creating.

Let us see if this is not true.

If you believe a thing is so, is not that thing really so — to you?

Is it not true that a thing seems real to you, like some sin or evil, so-called, some sorrow, trouble or worry, only because your thinking or believing it so makes it such? Others might see that thing entirely differently and might think your view of it foolish. Might they not?

If this is true, then your body, your personality, your character, your environment, your world, are what they appear to be to you, because you have thought them into their present status.

Therefore you can change them by the same process, if they do not please you; you can make them whatever you will, by thinking them so. Can you not?

But how can one do real thinking, conscious thinking, so as to bring about this change? You ask.

First know that I, *your Real Self*, purposely brought to your attention these things which now are displeasing and which cause you to think them as being what they now seem to be to you. I, and I alone, AM thus preparing your human mind so that, when you turn within to Me in abiding Faith and Trust, I can enable you to see and bring into outer manifestation the *Reality* of these things which now seem so unsatisfactory.

For I bring to you everything that, by its outer seeming, can attract or lure your human mind onward in its earthly search, in order to teach you of the illusoriness of all outer appearance of material things to the human mind, and of the fallibility of all human understanding; so that you will turn finally within to Me and My Wisdom, as the One and Only Interpreter and Guide.

When you have turned thus within to Me, I will open your eyes and cause you to see that the only way you can ever bring about this change in thinking, is by first changing your attitude toward all these things you now think are not what they ought to be.

That is, if they are unsatisfactory or obnoxious to you and affect you so as to cause you discomfort of body or disturbance of mind, — why, *stop thinking* that they can so affect or disturb you.

For who is the master? Your body, your mind, or You, the I AM within?

Then why not show You are master, by thinking the true things the I AM of you within wishes you to think?

It is only by your *thinking* these other things, by allowing these inharmonious thoughts to enter your mind and by so doing *giving them the power* so to affect or disturb you, that they have any such influence over you. When you stop thinking into them this power, and *turn within to Me and allow Me to direct your thinking*, they will at once disappear from your consciousness, and dissolve into the nothingness from which your created them by your thinking.

When you are willing to do this, then and then only are you ready to receive Truth, and, by proper conscious thinking, directed by Me, to create the true and permanent things I within wish you to create.

Then, when you can thus distinguish the true from the false, the real from the seeming, your conscious thinking will be as potent to create all things you desire, as has been your unconsciousness thinking in the past in creating those things you once desired but now find obnoxious.

For it was by your unconscious thinking, or thinking unconscious of the control your desires exercised over your creative power, that your world and your life are now what you sometime in the past desired them to be.

Have you ever studied and analyzed the process of the working of your mind when a new Idea fertile with possibilities appears?

Have you noticed the relation that Desire bears to such an Idea, and how, through thinking, that Idea is finally brought to actual fruition?

Let us study this relation and process.

There is always first the Idea, not considering at this moment the necessity or occasion for Its appearance. It matters not whence the Idea comes, from within or without; for it is always I who inspire It or cause It to impress your consciousness at the particular moment it does.

Then, just to the extent that you grow quiet and focus your attention upon that Idea, stilling all the activities of your mind and eliminating all other ideas and thoughts from your consciousness, so that Idea can have full sway, do I illumine your mind and cause to unfold before your mental gaze the various phases and possibilities contained within that Idea.

This takes place, however, up to this point, without any volition on your part, other than focusing or concentrating your attention upon the Idea.

Once I have given your human mind a view of Its possibilities, and have enlisted your interest, then does your human personality take up its task; for as I created and inspired the Idea in your mind, so did I cause that Idea to fructify therein and give birth to Desire, desire to bring into outer manifestation all the possibilities of the Idea, Desire thus becoming the mortal agent of My Will and supplying the motive Power; just as the human personality is the mortal instrument used to confine and focus that Power.

Yes, all ideas and all desires come thus from Me. They are My Ideas and My Desires which I inspire in your mind and heart in order to bring them through you into outer manifestation.

You have no ideas of your own and could not possibly have a desire that came from other than Me, for I AM all there Is. Therefore all desires are Good, and when thus understood unfailingly come into speedy and complete fulfillment.

You may wrongly interpret My Desires, My Urges from within, and seek to use them for your own selfish purpose, but even while permitting this they still fulfill My Purpose. For it is only by letting you misuse My Gifts and by the suffering such misuse brings, that I can make you into the clean and selfless channel I require for the perfect expression of My Ideas.

We have, then, first the Idea in the mind; then the Desire to bring the Idea into outer manifestation.

So much for the relation. Now for the process of realization.

In accordance with the definiteness with which the picture of the Idea is held in the mind, and the extent to which the Idea possesses the personality, does its creative Power, impelled by Desire, proceed with Its work. This It does by compelling the mortal mind to *think out* or to imagine (image in), or, in other words, to build mental forms into which I can pour, as into a vacuum, the Impersonal, elemental, vital substance of the Idea. When the Word is spoken, either silently or audibly, consciously or unconsciously, this substance at once begins to materialize Itself, by first directing and controlling the consciousness and all the activities of both mind and body, and of all minds and all bodies connected with or related to the Idea, for remember, all consciousness, and all minds and all bodies are Mine, and are not separated but are One and wholly Impersonal, —and then so attracting, directing, shaping and molding conditions, things and events that, sooner or later, the Idea actually comes forth into definite, tangible manifestation.

So it is that every thing, every condition, every event that ever transpired, was first an Idea in the mind. It was by desiring, by *thinking*, and by speaking forth the Word, that these ideas came into visible manifestation.

Think this out and prove it for yourself.

This you can do, if you will, by taking any Idea that comes and following it out through the above process to realization; or by tracing back any feat you have accomplished, any picture you have painted, any machine you have invented, or any particular thing or condition now existing, to the Idea from which it sprang.

This is the plan and process of all true thinking, and therefore of all Creation.

Listen! *You* have now and always have had, through this power of thinking, dominion over all the kingdoms of the earth. If you but know it. You have now, this moment, only to Think and SPEAK THE WORD, — realizing your power, and that I, God, your Omniscient, Omnipresent, Omnipotent Self, will bring about the results, and the waiting consciousness of the invisible cells of all matter upon which your will and attention become focused, —which waiting consciousness is My consciousness, remember, —will begin immediately to obey and do exactly according to the image or plans you have prepared by you *thinking*.

For all things are made by the Word, and without the Word was not anything made that was made.

When you can once realize this and can know that I AM Consciousness within you is one with the consciousness of all animate and inanimate matter, and that Its will is one with your will, which is My Will, and that all your desires are My Desires, then will you begin to know and feel Me within, and will acknowledge the Power and Glory of My Idea, which is eternally expressing Itself Impersonally through you.

But it is first wholly necessary that you learn *HOW* to think, how to know Your thoughts, those directed by Me, from the thoughts of others; how to trace thoughts back to their source and to banish undesirable ones at will from your consciousness; and finally how to control and *utilize* your desires so that they will always serve *YOU*, instead of your being a slave to them.

You have within you all possibilities. For I AM there. My Idea must express, and It must express through you. It will express itself perfectly if you but let it; if you will only still your human mind, put aside all personal ideas, beliefs and opinions, and let if flow forth. All you need to do is to turn within to Me, and *let Me direct your thinking* and your desires, let Me express whatever I will, you personally accepting and doing what I desire you to do. Then will your desires come true, your life become one grand harmony, your world a heaven and your self one with My Self.

When you have begun to realize this and have glimpsed somewhat of its inner meaning, then you will be ready to grasp the real import of what follows.

7

The Word

We will now take the Key and show you how the plan and process just described is the one by which the world came into existence, how the earth and all that is in it and on it, including yourself and your brothers and sisters, are but the outer manifestations on an Idea, My Idea, which is now being thought into life expression.

I, the Creator, AM the Original THINKER, the *One* and *Only* THINKER.

First know that.

As previously stated, man does not think. It is I Who think through his organism. Man believes he thinks, but before he has awakened to a realization of Me within he only takes the thoughts I attract to or inspire in his mind, and, mistaking their real meaning and purpose, places a *personal* construction upon them and, through the selfish desires thus aroused, creates for himself all his troubles and brings upon himself all his woes.

These apparent mistakes, misconstructions and interferences of man are in reality only the obstacles in his way to be overcome, that he may, through the overcoming, finally develop a body and mind strong and clean and capable enough to express perfectly and consciously this Idea of Mine eternally working within his Soul.

Man, then, is only the organism I AM thus preparing through which to manifest the perfection of My Idea. He provides the personality, with its body, mind and intellect, through which I can express this Idea perfectly, the physical brain with which I can think and speak It into outer manifestation.

I plant in man's brain an Idea — any idea. That idea would grow, mature and speedily ripen into complete outer fruition or manifestation, — if man only would let it, would give his mind and all its thoughts, his heart and all its desires wholly over to Me, and let Me come forth as the perfect fulfillment of that Idea.

I will now plant in your brain-mind an Idea. May It grow, mature and ripen into the glorious harvest of Wisdom which is awaiting you, — if you *let Me* direct Its growth and expression through you.

In one of My other Revelations, called the Bible, you are told much about "The Word" but very few, even the most learned Bible students, comprehend My meaning.

You are told that:

"In the beginning was the Word, and the Word was with God, and the Word was God. The same was in the beginning with God. All things were made by him, — by the Word, — and without Him — the Word — was not anything made that was made."

You shall learn herein how My Word was in the beginning, how It was with Me, and how It was I, My Self; how all things were made by Me and by My Word, and that without Me and My Word was nothing made that now exists.

Now, a word to the human understanding is a symbol of an Idea; that is, it stands for, embodies, and represents an Idea.

You are a Word, a symbol of an Idea, if you can see it. So is a diamond, a violet, a horse.

When you can discern the idea back of the symbol, then you know the soul or the reality of the manifestation *appearing* as a man, a diamond, a horse, a violet.

Hence, a word, as used in the above quotation, means an Idea, an Idea latent and unmanifest, however, waiting to be expressed, or thought and spoken forth, in some *form* or another.

The Word that was in the beginning and that was with Me was then not only an Idea, but It was *My* Idea of My Self *IN EXPRESSION* in a new state or condition, which you call earth life.

This Idea was I, My Self, because It was part of Me, being as yet latent and unmanifest within Me; for It was of the substance and essence of My *Bei-ng*, which is Itself an Idea, the One Original Idea.

All things were made by Me by the vitalized action of this, My Idea, being thought and spoken into expression; and nothing has been or ever can be expressed in earth life without having My Idea as the primary and fundamental cause and principle of its being.

This, My Idea, therefore, is now in the process of unfoldment or of being thought into outer expression some call it evolution, — just as is the flower when the bud puts forth from the stalk and finally opens into the blossom, obeying the urge to express My Idea hidden within its soul.

Just so will I develop and unfold all My mediums of expression, which shall finally, unitedly and completely picture forth My Idea from out their souls, in all the glory of Its perfection.

At present these mediums are of such nature that they require many languages of many types, from the simplest to the most complex, composed of almost an infinite number of Words, to express My Idea.

But when I shall have completely *thought* out My Idea, or shall have perfected My many mediums of expression, then shall My Idea shine forth in every Word, each, in fact, being a perfect part or phase of My Idea, all so chosen and arranged that they will really be as one Word, radiating the sublime significance of My Meaning.

Then shall all languages have melted, merged, into one language, and all words into One Word; for all mediums shall have become One flesh, the *now perfected medium* for the complete expression in One Word of My Idea, — My SELF.

Then shall My SELF, now capable of being expressed by these perfected Words, shine through Its medium of expression, — through the personalities, their bodies, minds and intellects; and *the Word shall have become flesh, or shall BE the flesh.*

This means that all Words, through the regenerative power of My Idea within, shall have evolved through the flesh, transmuting and spiritualizing it and making it so transparent and pure that the personality will have nothing more of earth nature left in it to *hinder* Impersonal expression, enabling My SELF, therefore, to shine forth perfectly and become fully manifest; thus amalgamating once more all Words and all flesh into One Word, *THE WORD, which was in the beginning,* and which then will shine through all created flesh as the SUN OF GLORY, — The CHRIST of GOD!

This is the *plan* and *purpose* of My Creation and of all manifested things.

A glimpse of the process of My Creation, or of My Thinking My Idea of My Self into Earth expression, will be given in what follows.

8

My Idea

You have been told that the Earth and all things belonging to it are but the outer manifestations of My Idea, which is now in the process of being thought into perfect expression.

You have been shown that My Idea is responsible for all created things, and that It is both the Cause and the Reason for all manifestations, yourself and your brothers and sisters included, all of which have been thought into existence by Me, the One Original Thinker and Creator.

We will now trace the course of that Idea from *the beginning*, through Its various stages of Earth expression, as well as the process of My Thinking that Idea into its present state of manifestation.

In the beginning, at the dawn of a new Cosmic Day, when the Word consciousness was just awakening and the stillness of Cosmic Night yet prevailed, I The THINKER, conceived My Idea.

This My Idea of My Self in manifestation in a new condition, called Earth expression, I saw completely pictured in the mirror of My Omniscient Mind. In this mirror I saw the *real* Earth shining forth brilliantly in the Cosmos, —a perfect Sphere, where all the Infinite phases, attributes and powers of My Divine Nature were finding perfect expression through the medium of Angels of Light, living Messengers of My Will, My Word in the Flesh, even as It is in the Celestial World of the Eternal.

I saw My Self manifesting outwardly as Nature, and My Life as the vivifying and evolving Principle back of all Manifestation. I saw Love, the Divine Creative Power, as the animating and vitalizing Force back of all Life, and My Desire to give perfect expression to that Love as the Potential and Real Cause and Reason of the birth of My Idea.

All this I saw mirrored in My All-seeing and All-knowing Mind, which could see and reflect only the Soul of things or their Reality. Therefore this that I saw pictured in My Mind was the Real Earth, in fact, its *beginning*, its *conception* into Cosmic being.

Now, My Consciousness is the inner essence of all Space and all Life. It is the real Substance of My All-comprehending and All-including Mind, whose informing and vitalizing Center is everywhere and Its limit and circumference nowhere. *Within the realm of My Mind alone* I live and move and have My *Be-ing*. It both contains and fills all things, and Its every vibration and manifestation is but the expression of some phase of My *Be-ing*.

Be-ing is ex-pressing or out-pressing. You cannot imagine being without expression. Therefore, I, All that is, AM expressing, constantly and continuously expressing.

Expressing what?

What else could I express, if I AM All that Is, but My Self?

You cannot yet see or comprehend when I inspire you with an Idea.

Therefore, if I AM All there is, that Idea, which is direct from Me, must be part of or a phase of My Self in Being or Expression.

Any Idea, once born within the realm of *My Mind*, as has been shown, immediately becomes a Reality, for in the Eternality of My Being Time is not. With you, however, an Idea first creates Desire, a desire to express that Idea; then

Desire compels Thinking, Thinking causes Action, and Action produces Results —the Idea in actual outer manifestation.

In Reality I have no Desire, for *I AM All Things*, and All Things are *of* Me. I need only to think and Speak the Word to produce results.

Yet that Desire you feel in you is from Me, because it is born of My Idea, which I implanted in your mind only that It might come forth into expression through you. Indeed, whatever you desire is I, knocking at the door of your mind, announcing My Purpose of manifesting My Self in you or through you in the particular form indicated by that Desire.

What is called Desire in human personalities, is but the necessary Action of My Will pushing forth the expression of My Idea into outer Manifestation or Being.

What to you would seem to be in Me a desire for expression, is but the Necessity of My Idea of My Self to Be, or Express Itself.

Therefore, every *real* desire you feel, every desire of *your heart*, comes from Me and must of necessity sometime, in some shape or other, be fulfilled.

However, as I have no Desire, because I AM All Things, once this Idea of expressing My Self in this new condition was born, I had but to *think*, that is, to concentrate or focus My Attention upon My Idea and Will It to come forth into expression, or, as is told in My other Revelation, to Speak the Creative Word, and at once did the Cosmic Forces of My Being, set in vibration by the concentrating of My Will, proceed to attract the necessary elements from the eternal storehouse of My Mind, and, with My Idea as a nucleus, to combine, form and shape around It these elements into what is called a thought-form of a planet, filling it with My Life Substance — My Consciousness — and endowing it with all the potentialities of My Being.

This act of thinking produced only a vitalized *thought-form* of a planet, and its manifestation was still in a nebulous state in the thought realm.

From a thought-form, however, the quickening power of the Idea within, with My Will focused upon It, proceeded to mold, fashion and gradually to solidify into material form the various elements of Life Substance; until My Idea finally shone forth in substantial manifestation in the world of visible forms as the planet Earth, a medium ready for living expression, and now capable of both containing and expressing Me.

This was the material body prepared by My Thinking, in which already dwelt all the potential nature of My Being, by reason of the informing power of My Idea within.

The next stage was the developing and preparing of avenues or mediums through which I could express the manifold phases, possibilities and powers of My Idea.

The outward evidence of this was what is known as the mineral, vegetable and animal kingdoms, which, each in turn, as it came into manifestation, gradually unfolded higher and more complex states of consciousness that enabled Me more and more clearly to express the infinite phases and variety of My Nature.

It was at this stage that I looked upon My Creation, as stated in My other Revelation, and saw that It was good;

But there yet remained the final and culminating medium of expression.

Up to this point, while each perfectly expressed some phase of My Nature, yet all existing mediums and avenues were unconscious of Me, and were mediums of expression only as a wire is a medium for conducting heat, light and power.

The conditions were ripe, however, for the creation of mediums through which My Divine Attributes could find conscious expression, conscious not only of their relationship to Me, but of their ability and power to express My Idea.

It was at this moment in Time that You and Your Brothers and Sisters were born into existence as human expressions, coming into manifestation as you did, similarly with all other mediums, in response to My concentrated Thought, in which I saw all the infinite variety of My Attributes in actual expression in entitized[1] forms, each manifesting in predominance some particular phase of My Being, and each conscious of Me, Its Creator and Expressor.

I saw *You* in perfect expression, even as I see You now the *Real You*, an *Attribute* of My Self perfect.

For in Reality You are an Angel of Light, one of My Thought Rays, an Attribute of My Being, ensouled in Earth conditions, with no other purpose (which is no purpose at all, but a necessity of My Being) but the final complete expression of My Idea.

In the Eternal there is no Time, or Space, or Individuality, and it is only by reason of the phenomenon of Thought being born from the womb of Mind into the world of Matter that the illusions of Time, Space and Individuality occur; the thought, or Creature, acquiring the consciousness of separateness from its Thinker or Creator.

So it was then that the first tendency to *think* yourself as separate from Me was born. The complete consciousness of separation did not become established until long after.

In the beginning, when You thus first entered into Earth expression, obeying the impulse I had sent forth through My concentrated Thought, You, one of My Attributes, surrounded or clothed Your Self with My Idea of My Self in expression as

---

[1] Converted from one form to another; Intentionally, actively perceived as alive -

the particular Attribute You represented. You being the animating Force of that Idea.

In other words, My Idea of My Self expressing that particular Attribute then became the Soul of Your particular expression. But that Idea or Soul is not You, remember, for You are really a part of Me, being *My Self* in expression through the medium of that particular Attribute.

Having clothed Your Self with My Idea, this Idea then, through the necessity of Its being, immediately began to attract to Itself the necessary *Thought Substance* requisite for the expression of that particular Attribute, and to build and shape it into My Image and Likeness. It thus became a Holy Temple, filled with My living Presence, because inhabited by You, one of My Divine Attributes.

This Temple, being in My Image and Likeness, and composed of My Thought Substance, surrounding and clothing My Idea, is consequently your *Real* body. It is therefore indestructible, immortal, *perfect*. It is My complete, imagined (imaged in) Thought, containing My Living Essence, awaiting the time when it can come into outer expression and take on material form.

So now we have:

- First, *I AM*, expressing as *You*, one of My Divine Attributes;

- Second, *My Idea* of You, one of My Attributes, expressing in Earth conditions— or Your Soul;

- Third, My Imaged Thought of You, forming the Temple of *Your Soul* —or Your Soul Body in which You dwell.

These three make up the Divine or Impersonal part of You, the Immortal *Three–in–One* — You, My latent yet completely formulated thought, shaped in My Image and Likeness, as yet unquickened, and therefore having no connection with your human personality, which has not yet been born.

9

The Garden *of* Eden

Whether or not you have gotten any clear grasp of what has just been stated, do not discard it as impossible of comprehension. For in every line is hidden a meaning that will more than repay you for the study necessary to make it become clear.

This Message is to awaken you to a realization of what You are, to a realization of your *real* Self. It is intended to make you once more conscious of Me, your Divine Self, so conscious that never again will you be deceived by that other self, which you have imagined as being you and which so long has lured you on by feeding you with its unsatisfying sense pleasures, its mental dissipations and emotional delights.

Before that can be it will be necessary for you thoroughly to know that supposed other self, that self which You created by *thinking* it real and separate from Me, and then kept alive by giving it the power thus to entice and deceive you; yes, that self-created self, with its purely selfish pride and ambitions and imagined power, its love of life, of possessions, of being thought wise or good, — but which self is merely your human personality, which was born only to die as a separate identity, and as such has no more reality or permanence that the leaf, the snow or the cloud.

Yes, you will be brought face to face with that petty personal self, and will see with perfect vision all its sordid selfishness and human vanities; and you will then learn if you but turn to Me and ask in simple faith and trust that it is I, the

Infinite, *Impersonal* part of You, abiding always within, Who am thus pointing out to you all these illusions of the personality, which for so many ages have separated you in consciousness from Me, Your glorious, Divine Self.

This realization will surely come, when you can recognize that this Message is from Me, and when you have determined that it shall be. To you, whom I have inspired with such a determination, I will cause every illusion in time to disappear, and you shall in truth *know* Me.

The exercise of your mind along these abstract lines will not hurt you. Instead it is what your mind needs. For, not until you can grasp My Meaning when presented to you in ideas such as there herein contained, coming from without, can you perceive and correctly interpret My Idea when I inspire you from within. Your mind I AM thus preparing for USE, not to gain more earthly knowledge, but in order that you can receive and give *forth* My Heavenly Knowledge to those whom I shall bring to you for that purpose.

With a prayer to Me, Your Own Real Self, your Father-in-Heaven, that true realization may come, read carefully what follows.

We have arrived, in the course of our consideration of the process of unfoldment of My Idea, to where the I AM of you, manifesting in your Immortal Soul Body, or in the Thought Image created by My Thinking, is now ready to take on a substantial form, a form suitable for the Earth expression of My Attributes.

This change from a mental to a mortal form took place after the manner and process of all thinking and creating, and is literally described in the Bible, where it says I "formed man of the dust of the ground, and breathed into his nostrils the breath of life; and man became a living soul."

Shall I explain further? — That the quickening power within My Idea (your Soul) proceeded to attract to it the various elements of life substance (dust), and, atom by atom, and cell by cell, in due course of time, to mold and shape each into substantial reality, after the pattern of the Thought Image composing your Soul Body, thus forming an Earthly outer covering, as it were, — until finally your mortal form actually became manifest to the psychic sense, if not yet to what is called the physical sense. Whereupon, all being now prepared for this cyclic moment, *You*, My Attribute, breathed into and then through its nostrils (from within) the breath of life, and You then made your first appearance of Earth as a *human being* — a *living* Soul (My Idea now able to express consciously through a suitable Earth medium), containing within your Self all of My Attributes, all of My Powers and all of My Possibilities.

Thus were now manifest all the various mediums for the Earth expression of My Idea; and You, being one of My Attributes, naturally had dominion over all of these mediums, or possessed the power of utilizing any or all of them, if necessary, for the full and complete expression of *Your* — My Attributes — powers and possibilities.

In this manner and for this reason alone did You and Your Brothers and Sisters come into human expression. While in human form yet Your expression was so entirely Impersonal, that, though self-conscious, you still looked wholly to Me within for inspiration and guidance.

This, then, was the first condition into which You awakened when You entered into Earth expression, and is what is called the Edenic state or dwelling in the Garden of Eden.

This Edenic state represents the Celestial phase of Impersonal Consciousness, or that state in which You were still consciously One with Me, though now confined in a mortal medium of expression.

Now, I shall not tell you in detail how or why it became necessary for Me to "drive" You (now manifesting as Man or Humanity) out of the Garden of Eden, other than to remind you of the part that Desire plays in Earth expression, and its relation to My Will; how it centers your interest in outer things and makes you forget Me within.

When you have solved that and comprehended somewhat of My reason, then perhaps you can understand the necessity of first causing You (Humanity) to fall into a deep sleep (You having arrived at the close of another Cycle called a Cosmic day), and of letting you dream you had awakened, but in reality you were and are *still asleep*, and everything from that day to this, including all seeming earthly events and conditions, have been but a Dream, from which you will fully awaken only when You (Humanity) again become wholly conscious of Me within, — and of finding Yourself (Humanity) no longer outwardly one, but two; one an active, thinking, aggressive part, thereafter called a man, and the other a passive, feeling, receptive part, — a womb-man, or woman;

Also the necessity of these seeming earth influences being brought to bear to draw Your consciousness from purely Celestial delights and to hold it in this new Dream condition, in order to develop a mortal mind, that You might through its natural selfish tendencies become centered entirely upon Your Earthly mission of mortal expression;

And the wisdom of having this influence, through the Serpent of Selfishness (the shape I caused it to assume in your mind), first generate in the passive, feeling, receptive part of You Desire, the mortal agent of My Will, which was to supply the motives and the power for the further and complete expression of My Attributes on Earth;

And finally the necessity of Desire casting its complete spell over You (Humanity), that Your Celestial or Impersonal nature might be kept deep in sleep; until, in your Dream, by the free but ignorant use of My Will, You could taste and fully eat of the *fruit* of the so-called Tree of Knowledge of Good and Evil, and through the eating could learn properly to discriminate and know its fruit for what it really is; and thus acquire the strength to use the knowledge thus gained wisely and perfectly in the expression of My Idea only.

You likewise possibly now can understand how in your Dream you became more and more engrossed in and attached to this false earth state, through first eating of this fruit and learning to know Good and Evil, and after learning of the new and enticing world thus opened up to you, dying to the knowledge of the Reality back of it all; and how and why it was You learned that You were naked both the thinking and the feeling parts of You; and also why you grew afraid and tried to hide from Me, thus creating in your consciousness the sense of separation from Me.

Now, perhaps, you can see why this all had to be, why You (Humanity) had to leave the Edenic state of Impersonal Consciousness and lose Your Self wholly in the earth illusions of this Dream World, in order to be able to create a body and develop in it a personal or self consciousness capable of fully expressing My Perfection.

Thus was born Your human personality, and since its birth have I impelled You to nourish, support and strengthen it, by filling You with longings, hopes, ambitions, and aspirations, with all the various manifestations of Desire; which are but the human phases of My Will, operating in the preparation and development of a medium capable of expressing perfectly My Attributes on Earth.

And so I Spake the Word, and drove You out of the Garden of Eden, and clothed You with a "coat of skin," or, in other words, with flesh, the same as other animals. For now, in order that You might enter into the heart of Earth conditions, into the real Earth, the Earth of My Idea, — not the one of your Dream, so as to quicken My Idea therein into active life expression, You, My Attribute, had to have an organism and a covering appropriate to the conditions in which You were to manifest in your Dream.

Likewise, in thus giving You a coat of skin, did I, by so doing, provide My Idea with a suitable form for Earthly expression, I gave you the power to express Your Self, through a definite organism, by means of words.

In the Impersonal there is no use or necessity for words. Ideas alone exist and express. They simply *Are*, for they are the expression of the various phases of My *Be-ing*.

But in this Dream condition, where every expression in these early stages of outer being had to have a form and substance that could be heard, seen, felt, smelled or tasted, in order that its meaning could be clearly apprehended, there naturally had to be provided organisms capable of being used for the double purpose of expression and of understanding what was expressed.

As My Idea unfolded Itself, after Your expulsion from Eden, You — one of My Divine Attributes, dwelling within My Idea of that Attribute in expression, in turn dwelling within the Thought Image of My Self, and finally manifesting outwardly in the Earth form of Words, when impelled by My Will in the guise of Desire to express My Meaning — began rapidly to "increase and multiply."

In Your search for the most favorable conditions for the manifestation of Your particular attributes, You gradually spread over the face of the Earth, each containing many words, and all born of Desire in the human mind to express in Earthly terms the infinite phases of My Idea ever surging within.

The more the *human* mind strove thus to express "in Words" My Idea, the greater and more abject the failure.

In time will the Great Awakening come that all Words are but Symbols of One Idea, and all Ideas of whatsoever nature are but phases of One Idea, My Idea of My Self in Expression, — and that all Desire to express in Words that Idea, without the consciousness of My Will being the One and Only source of Inspiration, is futile. Likewise, all desire to express that Idea in *living acts*, without losing all consciousness of your human personality — of your personal part in the acts, and centering your self wholly in Me, — is vain and fruitless and will end only in failure, disappointment and humiliation.

10

Good *and* Evil

I n the Garden of Eden, where you abode before entering upon your Earthly mission, there grew this tree whose fruit is called the Knowledge of Good and Evil.

While dwelling in the Garden you were still wholly Impersonal, for you had not yet tasted of this fruit. Having once yielded to Desire, the Earthly agent of My Will, whose main work is to make you eat this fruit, the moment you had eaten, that moment you descended, or fell, or were forced from your Edenic estate (like the chick from the shell or the rose from the bud), and you found yourself involved in conditions altogether new and strange. For now, instead of having dominion over the lower kingdoms, and of their supplying your every want, you had to till the ground to get it to bring forth fruit, and by the sweat of your brow had you to earn your bread.

Having taken upon yourself this Earthly mission, it now became necessary for you to enter fully into all conditions of Earth life, in order to develop a mind and perfect a body capable of expressing perfectly My Idea on Earth, — the real cause and reason of your entering into this Dream condition.

So having fallen or stepped out of your Impersonal or Edenic estate, you yielded completely to the lure of this Dream World, and now permitting Desire wholly to lead, you no longer were capable of seeing the Reality or Soul of things; for you had put on a physical body, an earthly covering with a human brain, which acted as a veil to your Soul Consciousness, and so bedimmed your sight and clouded your mind that the light of Truth did not penetrate through, and everything was falsely colored and distorted by your human understanding.

In this Dream condition you saw all things darkly, as through a mist, and with this mist enshrouding everything you could not see things in their Reality, but only their misty *appearance*, which now however seemed to you the *real* things themselves.

This was so with everything you saw through your Dream eyes, with things both animate and inanimate, with everything you conceived in your human mind, with even your own Self and your other Selves round about you.

Thus no longer seeing the Soul of things, but only their misty shadows, you grew to thinking these shadows were real substance, and that the world about you was composed of and filled with such substance.

This mist was only the effect of the Light of Truth being invisible to your human mind, whose intellect, like an imperfect lens, only befogged and twisted everything and made it appear as Real, keeping your consciousness continually busied with these myriad illusions of your Dream World.

Now the intellect is a creature of and wholly controlled by Desire, and is not, as many suppose, a faculty of the Soul. In other words, this mist then was the clouded lens of your human intellect, which, because controlled by Desire, falsely portrayed and interpreted to your consciousness every image, idea and impulse I inspired from within or attracted from without, during the process of My awakening your consciousness to a recognition of My Idea within ever urging for outer expression.

All this I did purposely, however, through the agency of Desire, in order to lead you consciously into the heart of Earth conditions.

While this false vision, inspired by Desire, caused many missteps and much trouble and suffering, and you gradually lost confidence in your Self — in Me, the Impersonal One within, in fact, you forgot Me, so that you did not know where to turn in your helplessness; yet it was only through your thus losing the memory of your Divine estate, and centering all your consciousness in these earthly conditions, that I could develop your human mind and will, and all your faculties, and provide your human body with the strength and powers that would enable Me to give perfect expression to My Divine Idea on Earth, which eventually must BE.

So, through your mistakes and troubles and sufferings, Desire for relief caused the Idea of Evil to spring up in your mind, and likewise when these troubles were not It inspired the Idea of Good.

To all *appearances* of things and conditions you attributed these qualities of Good or Evil, — according to whether or not they satisfied Desire My Agent, in Reality My *human Self,* or *You,* in your human personality.

All these conditions and experiences in life which you entered into, and which when pleasing seemed Good, and when displeasing seemed Evil, were merely incidents created by Desire to quicken in you certain Soul faculties, which would enable you to recognize the Truths that I, within wished at the time to impress upon your consciousness. The apparent Evil was the negative aspect of the Fruit of the Tree, which always lured you on by its fair appearance and by the sweetness of the first taste to eat and enjoy to satiation, or until its harmful effects manifested and became a curse, bringing final disillusionment; which served to turn or force you back in humiliation to Me, your True Self, Who, through the new consciousness thus aroused, was then enabled to extract the

Essence of the Fruit and incorporate it into Soul substance and tissue.

Likewise the apparent Good was the positive aspect of the Fruit, which, having pushed forth of itself into expression, through your recognition of and obedience to its urge, was now permitting you to enjoy its happy and natural *effects*, and to receive the outward benefits of *My* loving inspiration and guidance.

This *you*, who was being led by Desire through all these experiences, was only your human personality, which the *Real* you was training and developing and preparing so it could become a perfect instrument for Your use in the expression of My Idea, ever seeking to manifest Its perfection in the flesh.

All this *You* did, not only compelling your human personality to eat but to live on the fruit of the so-called Tree of Knowledge of Good and Evil, until you had seen and known all the so-called Evil, and from living on and with it had discovered in it the germ of so-called Good, plucked it, lifted it up, and turned it right-side out; so that you from that time on knew that Good and Evil had no real existence, and were but relative terms descriptive of outside conditions looked at from different viewpoints, or were only different outer aspects of a central *inner* Truth, the *Reality* of which was what You sought to Know, Be and Express.

During the latter ages you have been, as it were, gradually throwing off layer after layer of human consciousness, dissipating the mist or glamour thrown around your mind by the intellect; subduing, controlling, spiritualizing, and thus clarifying the intellect itself; until now you are beginning to awaken and to see, through the ever thinning remaining layers, occasional glimpses of Me, the one Great Reality, within all things.

All this time, *You*, the omniscient, Impersonal I AM of You, were consciously and intentionally doing all this; not for the purpose of getting the mere knowledge of earth conditions and things, as your Intellect has so loudly and authoritatively proclaimed, but in order that you might harvest what You had sown in the dim ages past, and could manifest My Perfect Idea on Earth, even as You are now manifesting It in the Impersonal estate, Your Heavenly Home.

You, remember, are the Great Impersonal I, Who AM doing all this, Who AM continually changing in outward appearance, but Who within AM eternally the same.

The endless flow of the Seasons, — the Spring, with its busy sowing; the Summer, with its warm, restful ripening; the Autumn, with its bounteous harvesting; the Winter, with its cool, peaceful plenty, year after year, life after life, century after century, age after age — are only the out-breathing of My Idea as I inspire It forth through the Earth and through You, My Attribute, and through all My other Attributes, during the process of unfolding in outer manifest state the perfection of My Nature.

Yes, I am doing it through You, because You are an expression of Me, because only through You, My Attribute, can I express My Self, can I BE. I AM expressing My SELF.

I AM in You as the oak is in the acorn. You are I as the sunbeam is the Sun. You are a phase of Me in expression. You, one of My Divine Attributes, are eternally trying to express My perfection through Your mortal personality.

Just as an artist sees in his mind the perfect picture he wants to paint, but his hand cannot quite portray with the crude mediums of brush and color the true quality and effect he sees, so do You see Me within Your Self and know We are One, but always are prevented, by the imperfection of the earthly material of your human personality, with its animal body, its mortal mind, and selfish intellect, from perfectly expressing Me.

Yet, I created your body, mind and intellect, in order to express My Self through you. The body I made in the Image of My Perfection; the mind I gave to inform you of Me and My works; the intellect I gave to interpret My Idea as I inspired it to the mind. But you have been so distracted by the *human* phases of this body, mind and intellect, and their outer uses, that you have forgotten Me, the One and Only Reality within, Whose Divine nature I AM ever seeking to express to and through you.

The time is soon here when the outward uses shall no longer distract, and My Reality shall be revealed unto you in all the glory of Its perfection *within* You.

You, when I thus reveal My Self, shall not be more blessed than before, unless that which I have revealed shall become the Bread of Life to you, and you shall live and *manifest* the Life It reveals.

11

Use

Now I have purposely not stated clearly all the how and why of these things; for I have reserved for you, when you call upon Me so to do, and are capable of receiving it, an inspiration *from within* with a far more comprehensive vision of the unfoldment and development of My Divine Idea, and Its final perfected expression, than is herein pictured.

If I were here to tell the *real* meaning of My many manifestations, before you were consciously capable of experiencing its Truth, you neither would believe My words, nor could you comprehend their inner application and use.

Therefore, as I begin to awaken in you a realization that I AM within, and more and more cause your human consciousness to become an Impersonal channel through which I can express, will I gradually reveal to you the Reality of My Idea, dissipating one by one the illusions of the ages which have hidden Me from you, enabling Me thereby to manifest through you My Heavenly Attributes of Earth in all their humanly Divine perfection.

I have herein given you but a glimpse of My Reality, but just to the extent that that which has been revealed becomes clear will more be opened up unto you from *within*, and far more wonderful than this now seems to you.

For My Idea within, when It finally and completely shines through Its mantle of flesh, will compel you to worship and glorify Me far above all that your human mind and intellect now conceive of as God.

Before you can become conscious of all this and can truly comprehend it, you and your human personality must make it possible for Me to reveal it, by turning within to Me as the *One* and *Only* Source, bringing to Me your measure absolutely empty of self, and with mind and heart as simple and trusting as those of a child.

Then and then only, when nothing of the personal consciousness remains to prevent My filling you full to overflowing with the consciousness of Me, can I point out to you the glories of My Real Meaning, for which this whole Message is but the outer preparation.

The time has now arrived, however, for you to comprehend somewhat of this. Enough has been revealed to prepare you for the recognition of My Voice speaking within.

Therefore, I shall now proceed as if you realize I AM within, and that these Truths which I voice through the medium of these pages are but to impress more strongly upon your consciousness those phases of My Idea which you could not clearly receive direct.

That which herein appeals to you as Truth is consequently but a confirmation of that which My Idea has heretofore been struggling to express from within.

That which does not appeal and which you do not recognize as your own, pass by, for that means I do not desire you to receive it as yet.

But each Truth I voice herein will go on vibrating until It reaches the minds I have quickened to receive It; for every word is filled with the potent power of My Idea, and to minds that perceive the Truth hidden therein this Truth becomes a living Reality, being that phase of My Idea they are now worthy and capable of *expressing*.

As all minds are but phases of My Infinite Mind, or parts of It manifesting in different forms of mortal nature, when I speak through the medium of these pages to your mind and to other minds, I AM but speaking to My mortal Self, thinking with My Infinite Mind, pushing forth My Idea into earthly expression.

Just so will You soon be thinking My Thoughts, and be conscious that I AM speaking within directly to your human consciousness, and you will then no longer have to come to this or to any other of My outer Revelations, either spoken or written, in order to perceive My Meaning.

For AM I not within You, and AM I not You, and are You not One with Me, Who live in and express through the consciousness of all minds, knowing all things?

All that remains for you to do is to enter into the All-consciousness of My Mind and abide there with Me, even as I abide within My Idea in Your Mind. Then all things shall be Yours, as they now are Mine, being but the outer *expression* of My Idea, and existing only by reason of the consciousness I gave them when I thought them into being.

It is all a matter of consciousness — of your conscious thinking. You are separated from Me only because you *think* you are. Your mind is but a focal point of My Mind. If you but knew it, what you call your consciousness is My Consciousness. You cannot even think, much less breathe or exist without My Consciousness being in you, — Can you not see it?

Well, then, *think*, believe you are I, that We are not separated, that We could not possibly be separated; for WE are ONE, — I within You, and You within Me, Think this is so; determinedly image it as so; and verily the moment you *are conscious* of this, that moment are you with Me in Heaven.

You are what you believe you are. Not one thing in your life is Real or has any value to you only as your thinking and believing has made it such.

Therefore, *think* no more you are separated from Me, and *abide* with Me in the Impersonal Realm, where all Power, all Wisdom, and all Love, the threefold nature of My Idea, but await expression through You.

Now I have spoken much of this, and have apparently said the same thing more than once, but in different words. I have done this purposely, presenting My Meaning in different lights, that you might finally be brought to comprehend My Divine Impersonality, which is in Reality *Your* Impersonality.

Yes, I have repeated and will continue to repeat many Truths, and you may think it tedious and unnecessary; but if you will read carefully you will find that each time I repeat a Truth I always add something to what has already been said, and that each time a stronger and more lasting impression is made upon your mind.

This done, My purpose has been accomplished, and you will soon come into a *Soul* realization of that Truth.

If you receive not such impression and still think such repetition a useless waste of words and time, know that your intellect only is reading, and that My *real* meaning has altogether escaped you.

You, however, who do comprehend, will love every word, and will read and reread many times, and consequently will receive all the wondrous Pearls of Wisdom I have held in reserve for you. These words and their message will be to you hereafter merely a fount of inspiration, or a door through which you will be enabled to enter into the Impersonal estate and to hold sweet communion with Me, your Father in Heaven, when I will teach you all things you desire to know.

I have been picturing the Impersonal estate from many viewpoints, in order that it may become so familiar that you can unerringly distinguish it from all inferior states, and may learn to dwell consciously in it at will.

When you can consciously dwell in it so that My Words when and wherever spoken can always find lodgment and understanding in your mind, then will I permit you to use certain faculties I have been awakening in you. These faculties will enable you more and more clearly to see the Reality of things, not only the beautiful and lovely qualities in the personalities of those about you, but their weaknesses, faults and shortcomings, as well.

But the reason you are enabled to see these faults and shortcomings, is not that you may criticize or judge your brother, but that I may arouse in you a definite resolve to overcome such faults and shortcomings in your own personality. For, mark you! — You would take no note of them in others were they not still in your self; for I within, then would not need to call them to your attention.

As all things are for *use*, and *use* only, let us study the use you have hitherto made of other faculties, gifts and powers I have given you.

You must realize by this time I have allowed you *all things*. All you have, or are, be it of good or evil, of blessing or suffering, of success or failure, of riches or lack, I have allowed you or attracted to you. — Why? For USE — in awakening you to a recognition and acknowledgment of *Me* as The Giver.

You could not honestly acknowledge Me as such until you *knew* I AM, The Giver. Your personality, in fact, had become so engrossed in trying to get rid of or to exchange many of the things I had given you for other things you thought were better, that of course you could not even dream, much less acknowledge, Me, *Your Own Self,* as The Giver.

Possibly you do now acknowledge Me as The Giver, as the Inner Essence and Creator of all things in your world and in your life, even of your present attitude toward these things.

Both are My doing, for they are but the outer phases of the process I AM using in the expression of My Idea of your inner Perfection, which Perfection being My Perfection is gradually unfolding from within you.

As you more and more realize this, will the true meaning and use of the things, conditions and experiences I send be revealed unto you. For you will then begin to glimpse My Idea within, and when you glimpse that Idea will you begin to *know* Me you own Real Self.

Before you can truly know Me, however, you must learn that all things I give you are Good — and that they are for *use*, My use, — and that you personally have no interest in or actual right to them, and they are of no real benefit to you, only as you put them to such use.

I may be expressing through you beautiful symphonies of sound, color or language, that manifest as music, art or poetry, according to human terminology, and which so affect others as to cause them to acclaim you as one of the great ones of the day.

I may be speaking through your mouth or inspiring you to write many beautiful Truths, which may be attracting to you many followers, who hail you as a most wonderful preacher or teacher.

I may even be healing through you diverse diseases, casting out devils, making the blind to see and the lame to walk, and performing other marvelous works which the world calls miracles.

Yes, all these I may be doing through you, but of absolutely no benefit is any of it to you personally, unless you use and apply these harmonies of sound in your every spoken word, so that to all hearers they will seem as the sweet music of heaven; and unless your sense of color and proportion so manifests in your life that only kind, uplifting, helpful thoughts flow from you, proving that the only true art is that of seeing clearly My Perfection in all My human expressions, and of allowing the quickening power of My Love to pour through you into their heart, picturing to their inner vision My Image hidden therein.

Likewise no credit attaches to you, no matter what wonderful Truths I speak or works I perform through you, unless you, yourself, live these Truths, daily, hourly; and make these works serve as a constant reminder of Me and My Power, which I ever pour out freely for you, My Beloved, and for all, to use in My Service.

You, to whom I have apparently given none of such gifts and who deem yourself unworthy and not yet advanced enough to serve Me in such ways, to you I would say:

Just to the extent that you truly recognize Me within and seek in real earnestness to serve Me, just to that extent will I use you no matter what your personality, no matter what its faults, tendencies and weaknesses.

Yes, I will cause even you who thus seek to serve Me to do many wondrous things towards the quickening and awakening of your brothers to a like acknowledgment of Me. I will cause even you to influence and affect the lives of many of those whom you contact, inspiring and uplifting them to higher ideals, changing their way of thinking and their attitude towards their fellows and therefore towards Me.

Yes, *all you* who seek to serve Me, no matter what your gifts, will I make to be a vital force for good in the community, altering the mode of life of many, inspiring and molding their ambitions and aspirations, and altogether becoming a leavening influence in the midst of the worldly activities in which I will place you.

You at the time will probably know nothing of this. You may even be still longing to serve Me, and hungering for a more intimate consciousness of Me, thinking you are doing nothing, are still making many mistakes and failing to live up to your highest ideals of Me; not realizing that this longing and hungering is the avenue through which I pour forth My Spiritual Power, which being wholly Impersonal, is used by you, unconscious of its being *I within you* using it, to bring about My Purpose in your heart and life and in the hearts and lives of My and Your other Selves.

So, as you finally grow into the realization of all this, as you surely will, and prove it by the practical use of all you have in My service, will I gradually give you the strength and ability to consciously to use Impersonally *My* Power, *My* Wisdom, and *My* Love, in the expression of My Divine Idea, which is eternally striving to manifest through You Its Perfection.

Therefore will you soon see that your human personality, with all its faculties, powers and possessions, which are in reality Mine operating and manifesting through you, is likewise for My use wholly, and that true success and satisfaction can never be found except in such use.

For such use develops, as the planted seed develops the harvest, the ability consciously to use *all* My Spiritual faculties in the final perfect expression of My Idea, which can be expressed only through your human personality.

12

Soul Mates

Let us now examine into some of the things I have given you, those especially of which you cannot yet acknowledge Me as the Giver. Perhaps the particular position in life you now occupy you do not think the best adapted for the expression of My Idea surging within you.

If so, then why not step out of that position into the one of *your* choice?

The mere fact that you cannot or do not do this proves that at this time such position is the one best suited to awaken in you certain qualities necessary for My perfect expression, and that I, your own Self, AM permitting you to remain therein, until you can recognize my Purpose and Meaning hidden within the power such position has to disturb your peace of mind and keep you thus dissatisfied.

When you recognize My Meaning and determine to make My Purpose your purpose, then and then only will I give you the strength to step out of that position into a higher I have provided for you.

Perhaps the husband or the wife you have, you think is far from being suited to you or capable of helping along your "spiritual" awakening, being only a hindrance and detriment, instead. You may even be secretly contemplating leaving or wishing you could leave that one for another who sympathizes and joins with you in your aspirations and seeking, and therefore seems more nearly your ideal.

You may run away if you will, but know that you cannot run away from your own personality; that, in selfish craving for a "spiritual" mate you may attract only one who will force you to a tenfold longer and harder search among the illusions of the mind, before you can again awaken to the consciousness of My Voice speaking within.

For a sympathetic and appreciative mate would only feed the personal pride and selfish desire for "spiritual" power in you, and develop further the egotistic side of your nature. Likewise, a loving, trusting, yielding mate might encourage only selfishness and conceit, when you are not yet abiding in the consciousness of My Impersonal Love; while a tyrannical, suspicious, nagging mate may provide the soul discipline you still need.

Did you but know it, the one who is your true Soul mate is in reality an Angel from Heaven, even as are You, one of the Attributes of My Divine Self, come to you to teach you that only when you have purged your own personality so that My Holy Love can express, can you be freed from any conditions which may now be causing you so much disturbance of mind and unhappiness of Soul.

For not until this Soul, this Angel from Heaven, this other part of My and Your Self, who has come to you and is yearning and striving to call into expression through you the Impersonal Love, the tender, thoughtful care for others, the poise of mind and peace of heart, the quiet, firm mastery of self, which and which alone can open the doors, so It can step forth into the freedom of Its own glorious Being and be to You Its own true Self, not until you can see this Soul in all Its Divine beauty, free of this earthly bondage, will it ever be possible for you to find and recognize that Ideal you seek.

For that Ideal exists, not without — in some other personality, — but only within, in your Divine Counterpart, which is I, your Higher, Immortal Self. It is only My Idea of this, your Perfect Self, striving to express and become manifest through your personality, that causes you to see seeming imperfections in the mate I have given you.

The time will come, however, when you cease to look without for love and sympathy, appreciation and spiritual help, and turn wholly to Me within, that these seeming imperfections will disappear; and you will see in this mate only the *reflection* of qualities of unselfish love, gentleness, trust, a constant endeavor to make the other happy, that will then be shining brightly and continuously from out your own heart.

Perhaps you cannot yet wholly believe all this, and you still question that I, your own Self, am responsible for your present position in life, or that I chose for you your present mate?

If so, it is well for you thus to question until all is made plain.

But remember, I will speak much more clearly *direct* from within, if you but turn trustingly to Me for help. For I ever preserve My Holiest secrets for those who turn to Me in deep, abiding Faith that I can and will supply their every need.

To you, however, who cannot yet do this, I say, if your own Self did not place you here or provide this mate, *Why* then are you here? And *Why* have you this mate?

Think!

I, the ALL, the Perfect One, make no mistake.

Yes, but the personality does, you say. And the personality chose this mate, and perhaps has earned no better position.

What, *who*, caused the personality to choose this particular one and earn this particular position in life? *Who* picked out and placed this one where you could thus choose, and who caused you to be born in this country of all countries and in this town of all towns in the world at this particular time?

Why not some other town and a hundred years later? Did your personality do all these things?

Answer truly and satisfactorily these questions to yourself, and you will learn that I God, within you, your own Self, do all things that you do, and I do them well.

I do them while expressing My Idea, Which is ever seeking manifestation in outer form as *Perfection* through you, My living Attribute, even as it is in the Eternal, within.

As for your true "Soul Mate," which you have been led by others to believe must be waiting for you somewhere, cease looking; for it exists not without in some other body, but within your own Soul.

For that within you which cries out for completion is only your sense of Me within, yearning for recognition and expression; Me, your own Divine Counterpart, the Spiritual part of you, your other half, to which and which alone you must be united, before you can finish what you came on Earth to express.

This is indeed a mystery to you who are not yet wedded in consciousness to your Impersonal Self; but doubt not, when you can come to Me in complete surrender, and will care for naught else than union with Me, then will I disclose to you the sweets of the Celestial Ecstasy I have long kept in reserve for you.

13

Authority

To you who still feel the desire to read books, thinking in them to find an explanation of the mysteries that now hide from you the meaning of the earthly expressions of My Idea, I say:

It is well that you seek thus outwardly, following the impulses I send, for others — interpretations of the meaning My Idea is expressing through them; for I will make that search to be of benefit to you, though not in the way you imagine.

It is even well for you to seek in ancient teachings, philosophies and religions, or in those of other races and other peoples, for the Truth I wish to express to you; for even that search will prove profitable.

But the time will come when you will realize that the thoughts of other minds and the teachings of other religions, no matter how true and beautiful, are not what I intend for you; for I have reserved for you thoughts and teachings which are yours and yours only, and which I will give to you in secret — when you are ready to receive them.

When the time comes, as it inevitably will, that you become dissatisfied in your search among the teachings of the various religions, philosophies and cults that now are interesting you, and you grow discouraged at finding yourself no nearer the attainment of the powers and spiritual growth so authoritatively described and supposedly possessed by the writers of the books, the teachers of the philosophies and the promulgators of the religions, — then will I show you that while all these books, teachings and religions were originally inspired by Me, and have done and are still doing their part in quickening the hearts of many, yet for you it is now meant that you cease looking to *any outer* authority, and instead confine your study to My Book of Life, guided and instructed by Me within, by Me alone. If you earnestly and truly do this, you will find that I have chosen you to be the High Priest of a religion, the glory and grandeur of which will be to all others that have been pictured to your former understanding, as the light of the Sun is to the twinkle of the far distant star.

You will likewise realize that the ancient religions were given to My peoples of long ages past, and that the religions of other races are for My peoples of those races, and that none of these are for you; even though I brought them to you and pointed out many wondrous things in them that inspired you to a more determined search for Me within their teachings.

I say to you, these are things of the past and have naught to do with you. The time has arrived, if you can see it, when you must cast aside all accumulated knowledge, all teachings, all religions, all authority, even My authority as expressed in this and My other *outer* revelations; for I have quickened you to the consciousness of My Presence *within*, to the fact that all authority, teachings and religions, coming from any *outer* source, no matter how lofty or sacred, can no longer have any influence with you, except as they become a means of turning you *within* to Me, for My *final* authority on all questions of whatsoever nature.

Therefore, why seek in the things of the past in religion, human knowledge, or in others' "experiences" for the help and guidance which I alone can give?

Forget all that has gone before. That which is past is dead. Why burden your soul with dead things?

Just to the extent you hold to things that are past, do you still live in the past, and can have naught to do with Me, Who dwell in the ever present NOW, the Eternal.

Just to the extent you attach yourself to past acts or experiences, religions or teachings, do they cloud your soul vision, hiding Me from you. They will ever prevent your finding Me until you free yourself of their darkening influence and step within, into the Light of My Impersonal Consciousness, which recognizes no limitations and penetrates to the infinite Reality of all things.

Likewise the future concerns you not. He who looks to the future for his final perfection is chained to the past and can never get free, until his mind no longer is thus engrossed with the consequences of his acts, and he recognizes Me as his only Guide and throws all responsibility upon Me.

You, who are one with Me, are perfect now, and always were perfect, knowing neither youth nor old age, birth nor death.

You, the Perfect, have naught to do with what has been or what is to be. You care not for anything but the eternal *NOW*. That only concerns you which immediately confronts you, — how perfectly to express My Idea here and now in the condition in which I have placed you purposely for such expression.

When that has been done, why not leave it behind, instead of dragging it along with you, burdening your mind and soul with consequences which are but empty shells from which you have extracted the meat?

All this applies to reincarnation, to which belief many minds are fast chained.

What have You, the Perfect, the Eternal, to do with past or future incarnations? Can the Perfect add to Its perfection? Or the Eternal come out of or return to eternity?

I AM, and You Are, — ONE with Me, — and always have been, and always will be. The I AM of You dwells in and reincarnates in ALL bodies, for the one purpose of expressing My Idea.

Humanity is My Body. In It I live, move and have My Being, expressing the Glorious Light of My Idea through My Attributes, whose Celestial Radiance to the human vision is bedimmed and distorted by the myriads of clouded and imperfect facets of the human intellect.

I and You, Who are One with Me, reincarnate in Humanity, as the oak reincarnates in its leaves and acorns, season after season, and again in the thousand oaks born from their thousands of acorns and their oaks, generation after generation.

You say you remember your past lives.

Do you? Are you *sure*?

Very well, what if you do? Just because I have permitted you a glimpse of the Reality of one of My past Expressions, that you might the better comprehend My Meaning which I am *now* expressing to you, is no assurance from *Me* that you *personally* were My Avenue of that expression.

For do I not express through all avenues, and You with Me, and are We not the Life and Intelligence of all expression, no matter what the character, or the age, or race?

If it pleases *you* to believe that you actually were that expression, it is well, and I shall cause such belief to be of benefit to you; but only to the extent of preparing you for the great Realization that afterward will come.

In the meantime you are chained fast. Your personality, with its selfish desires and selfish seeking, is still bound hand and foot to the past, and looks only to the future for its deliverance, after the final wearing out of all the consequences of its acts; dominating your mind and intellect with this false belief in birth and death, and that such is *your* only way to final emancipation and union with Me; preventing the realization of Our Eternal and Ever-Constant Oneness, and that You can free your Self any moment You will.

For it is only the personality that is born and dies, and which seeks and strives to prolong its stay in the body and in earth life, and then to return to other bodies after I no longer have any use for its body.

It is only to this personality that you are bound, by the benefits and opinions it has engrafted on you back through the ages, during which it has kept your human mind busied with such delusions. It is only when you can rise up in the realization of your Divine Immortality, Omnipotence and Intelligence, and can cast off *all* personal beliefs and opinions, that you can free your Self from this perverted relation, and can assume your true position as Master and King, One with Me, seated upon the Throne of SELF, compelling the personality to take its proper and natural place as servant and subject, ready and willing to obey My slightest command, thereby becoming an instrument worthy of My Use.

14

Mediums *and* Mediators

You, who, in your desire to serve Me, have joined yourself with a church, religious organization, occult society, or spiritual order, of whatsoever nature, thinking, by aiding in and supporting its work, it would please Me, and that you might receive special favors from Me in consequence, harken to these My Words and ponder over them.

First, know that I AM already pleased with you, for you do nothing that I do not cause you to do, and you do it to fulfill My Purpose, although it may seem to you at times you are acting contrary to My Wish and only to satisfy your own desires.

Know likewise that I provide all minds with all their experiences of life, which I utilize solely to prepare the body, quicken the heart and develop the consciousness, so that they can comprehend Me, and so that I can express through them My Idea.

I inspire minds with glimpses of Me and My Idea through these experiences, and I have spoken thus through inspiration to many, who have taken My Words and have written them in books and have taught them to other minds. These Words I have caused to quicken the hearts and consciousness of those who are ready to receive them, even though the writers and teachers of themselves had no real comprehension of My Meaning.

Many of those whose minds I thus inspire with glimpses of Me and My Idea I cause to become teachers and leaders, organizing churches and societies and cults, drawing seekers and followers to them, that I, through the words I speak through them, can quicken the hearts and consciousness of those that are ready to recognize Me.

I, the Impersonal One within, do all this, and the teachers and leaders personally do nothing, only serving as channels through which My Idea can express to the consciousness of those I draw to them for that purpose.

For the mind is only a channel and the intellect an instrument, which I use Impersonally wherever and whenever necessary to express My Idea. Not until the *heat* has been quickened and has opened wide to contain Me can man, with his mortal mind and intellect, consciously comprehend My Meaning, when I express through him My Idea.

You, in your desire to serve Me, may have found in some teacher or leader a personality whom you think, from the many seemingly wondrous words I speak through him, is now containing Me in his heart.

In your doubts and anxiety to please Me, and in your fear of My displeasure when disobeying My Commands, you may even have gone to such teacher or leader, who possibly claimed to be a priest or priestess of the Most High, thinking to get through such My Message to you, or words of advice or help from some "Master" or "Guide" you can hold. Until finally, in sorrow and humiliation from the disillusionment of which eventually and inevitably follows, you once more are thrown back upon yourself, upon the Teacher within, upon Me, your own True Self.

Yes, all the deception, all the discipline, all the taking of your ardor and devotion — not to speak of your money and services — to what you believe to be My Work, and selfishly purloining and utilizing them for the up-building and strengthening of their own personal power and prestige among their followers; feeding each of you with just enough subtle flattery and promises of spiritual advancement, together with clever sophistry under the guise of high and beautiful sounding spiritual teaching, to keep you bound to them so you would continue to support and honor and glorify them, ever holding over you the lash of My displeasure if they receive not unquestioning trust and obedience, — yes, all this I permit to be, for it is what you desire and seek, and Desire is truly the agent of My Will.

You may be even giving to some other teacher, — either in the seen or the unseen and no matter how true, well-meaning and spiritually wise,— who you think cannot be classed with the kind just mentioned, your unquestioning love, devotion and obedience, and you may be receiving what you think are teachings and guidance of inestimable value.

All this is well, so long as you are receiving that which you seek and think you need; for I supply all things to satisfy such desires. But know that all such is vain and unproductive of the real results sought; for all seeking and all desire for spiritual attainment is of the personality and therefore selfish, and leads only to final disappointment, disillusionment and humiliation.

If you but can see it, it is in the disillusionment and humiliation that the real results are attainable, for those are what I opened up for you and led you towards, when presenting the possibility of getting help from some human teacher; and these, disillusionment and humiliation, and what I purposely brought you to, in order that, having become once more humble and docile as a little child, you would then be ready to listen to and obey My Word spoken within, and, hearing and obeying, you could enter into My Kingdom.

Yes, all outward seeking will end thus, and will but bring you back to Me, weary, naked, starving, willing to listen to My Teaching and to do anything for even a crust of My Bread,

The Impersonal Life

which in your stubbornness and conceit you disdained before and deemed not good enough for your proud Spirit.

Now, if you have had enough of teachings and teachers, and are sure that within you lies the Source of all Wisdom, these words will bring joy unspeakable to your heart. For do they not confirm that which you already have felt *within* to be true?

For you who cannot yet see this and still need a Mediator, I have provided the story of The Christ crucified for your redemption, picturing how I desire you to live that, through the crucifixion of your personality, you may rise in consciousness to Oneness with Me.

But to you who are strong enough to bear it, I say you need no mediator between you and Me, for we are One already. If you can but know it, you can come direct and at once to Me in consciousness. I, God within you will receive you and you shall abide with Me for ever and ever; even as does My Son Jesus, the Man of Nazareth, through Whom I AM even now expressing as I did express two thousand years ago, and as I some day shall express through you.

To you who wonder how and why I say such beautiful and such spiritual things through personalities who fail to live up to the teachings they apparently of themselves give out, I say: I use all avenues Impersonally to express My Meaning.

Some I have prepared to be better mediums of expression than others, but personally knowing nothing of Me.

In some I have quickened the heart the better to contain Me, thereby becoming consciously more at One with Me.

Some have become so at One with Me that they no longer are separated in consciousness from Me, and in Them I live and move and express My Spiritual Nature.

Since the earliest days of expression on earth I have prepared My Priests and My Prophets and My Messiahs to

82

vision forth to the world My Idea — My Word that shall finally become flesh.

But whether I speak through Priest, Prophet or Messiah, or through a little child, or through your worst enemy, all words that appeal vitally to you are the words the I AM of *You* speaks through the organism of such medium to your Soul consciousness.

Should a number be gathered together to hear My Word spoken through one of My Priests, it is not the Priest of himself but *I, in the heart of each* hearer, Who draw from the Priest the vital words that sink deep into the consciousness of each. The Priest knows not what he says that so affects you, and may not even comprehend My Meaning of the words he speaks to you.

I within him do draw from the combined devotion to and belief in Me, consciously and unconsciously expressed by all those gathered around him, the Spiritual Force which serves as a channel or a connecting line through or over which I reach the consciousness of those minds I have prepared to comprehend My Meaning. For although I speak the same words to all, yet these words contain a distinct and separate message for each, and no one knows any but the message I speak to him; for I within you choose from the words the meaning I intend for you, and I within your brother and your sister likewise choose the meaning I intend for each of them.

When two or three are gathered together in My Name, there will I always be; for the Idea which draws them together I, within each, inspire – for it is My Idea. From the union of their aspirations towards Me do I create a medium or channel through which I enable the Soul consciousness to gain such glimpses of Me as each is capable of comprehending.

Every Priest, every Teacher, every Medium, I cause instinctively to know this, for they are My chosen Ministers;

and I likewise cause to awaken in them a desire to surround themselves with followers, that I may quicken, in the hearts of those who are ready a consciousness of My Presence within. The Priest, the Teacher, or the Medium, themselves, may never have recognized Me within, and may be deeming Me as entitized or personalized in some master or guide or savior without themselves; but nevertheless, there are those whom I lead to these, My Ministers, in whom, through certain words I cause My Ministers to speak, together with the Spiritual Force furnished by the various aspirants, I am enabled to awaken their Soul consciousness to a real comprehension of Me, the Impersonal One, seated *within* – in the very midst of All, in the heart of each.

For the I AM of My Minister, and the I AM of each follower are *One*, one in consciousness, one in understanding, one in love, and one in purpose, which purpose is the fulfillment of My Will.

This I AM, which is wholly Impersonal, and knows neither time, space nor different identities, merely utilizes the personalities of both Minister and followers, and the circumstance of personal contact, as a means of giving voice to My Idea, ever struggling within for outer expression.

Those Ministers who take the confidence and trust of My followers, and use it to further their own private purposes, I cause to awaken to a recognition of My Will and My Idea all in proper season. This awakening, however, is not pleasant to their personalities, and almost always causes much suffering and humiliation; but their souls rejoice and sing grateful praises to Me when I bring it to pass.

Therefore, wonder not at the sometimes wonderful words of Truth that come from mouths apparently unfit to speak them and comprehending not their meaning; nor at the fact that simple followers oftentimes awaken faster than and grow beyond their teachers. I Who dwell within both teacher and follower choose different conditions and provide different ways for the expression of My Attributes in each different Soul, fitting each into just the time and place where they can complement and help each other the best; thus uniting all into the most harmonious expression of My Idea possible under the circumstances.

15

Masters

You, who are still holding to the idea, taught in various teachings, that I will provide a "Master" or Divine Teacher for each aspirant towards union with Me, hear My Words.

It is true I have permitted you in the past to delve into all kinds of mystical and occult books and teachings, encouraging your secret desire to acquire the powers necessary to attain this union extolled in such teachings, even to the extent of quickening in you some slight consciousness of the possession of such powers.

I have even permitted the belief that by practicing certain exercises, breathing in a certain way, and saying certain mantrams, you might attract to you a "Master" from the unseen, who would become your teacher and help you to prepare for certain initiations that would admit you into an advanced Degree, in some secret Order in the inner planes of existence, where much of My Divine Wisdom would be opened up to you.

I have not only permitted these things, but, if you can see it, it was I who led you to these books, inspired in you such desire, and caused such belief to find lodgment in your mind; — but not for the purpose you imagine.

Yes, I have brought you through all these teachings, desires and beliefs, trying to point out to your human mind the Forces I use to bring into expression My Divine Idea.

I have portrayed these Forces as heavenly Hierarchies, and that your human intellect might the better comprehend, I pictured them as Angels or Divine Beings, Impersonal agents or executors of My Will, engaged in the process of bringing into expression My Idea that was in the beginning.

But you did not understand.

Your human intellect, enamored of the possibility of meeting and communing with one of these beings, as claimed in some of the teachings, proceeded at once to personalize Them, and began to long for Their appearance in your life, imagining that They are interested in your *human* affairs, and that by living in accordance with certain rules set down in certain teachings, you could propitiate Them so They would help you to gain Nirvana or Immortality.

Now I have purposely permitted you to indulge yourself with such delusions, letting you long, and pray, and strive earnestly to obey all the instructions given; even leading you on, sometimes, by giving you glimpses, in self-induced visions and dreams, of ideal beings, which I permitted you to believe were such "Masters."

I may even have caused to open in you certain faculties, which make it possible for you to sense the presence of personalities that have passed into the spirit side of life, and who have been attracted by your desires and seek to fulfill the part of Master and Guide to you.

Now the time has come for you to know that such beings are not Masters, also that Divine Beings do not call themselves Masters; that I, and I alone, your own Real Self, AM the only Master for you now, and until you are able to know Me also in your brother;—

That any being, either in human or spirit form, that presents himself to your consciousness and claims to be a Master, or *who permits you to call him Master*, is nothing more nor less than a personality, the same as yours, and therefore is not Divine, as your human mind understands that term, despite the many wonderful "truths" he may utter, and the "marvelous" things he may do.

Just so long as your human mind seeks or worships the idea of a Master in any other being, no matter how lofty or sacred he may seem to you, just so long will you be fed with such ideas; until, verily, I may perhaps, permit you to meet and commune with such a "Master."

If that "privilege" is vouchsafed you, it will be only in order to hasten your awakening and your consequent disillusionment, when you will learn that "Master" is indeed but a *personality*, — even though far more advanced in awakening than you, but still a personality and not the Divine One your innermost Soul is yearning for you to know.

For I feed you with every idea that will operate to teach you the reality back of the seeming, and if I lead you on to apparent deception and loss of faith in all human teachings, and in all human and even Divine perfection, it is only to enable you the more clearly to distinguish between the substance and the shadow, and to prepare you for that far higher Ideal I am waiting to picture to you.

You can rise in your human personality only to the ideal your *human* mind is capable of conceiving. Through Desire I cause My Will to manifest in you, and through Desire I perform many wondrous works.

If you doubt this, you need only to apply the Key;

To think of a Master is to create one.

This idea of a Master, by your thinking, becomes what you desire and imagine a Master to be.

In other words, by your thinking you build around this idea, all the qualities you imagine a Master possesses. Your human mind, through Desire, through aspiration, through worship, must needs create these qualities in some imaginary being, who is still a personality, for you cannot as yet conceive of an *Impersonal* being.

Therefore, according to the intensity of your desire and thinking, must this idea sooner or later come into actual manifestation, either by attracting to you such a personality in the flesh, or one entitized in the realm of visions and dreams.

As your human mind is constituted, it at certain times thinks it needs a Master, one to whom it can turn with its human trials and problems for explanation and advice, thinking life's problems can be settled that way. If I draw to you one who fails you or deceives you and throws you back finally upon Me, your own Self, discouraged, disillusioned and humiliated, it is only that perhaps then you will be ready to turn to Me within, and will listen to My Voice, which all these years has been speaking to you, but to which your proud and egoistic mind has not deigned to listen.

You who have not yet had this experience, who have not yet met the Master of your aspirations, either in human or spirit form; you, within whom My Words have failed to awaken a quickening response to their truth, — for you I have in store certain experiences which will surely lead you to Me later on, and then you will be brought to know that I AM the Master, the inspiring Idea back of and within every thought of and every aspiration towards a Master that enters your mind, whether coming from within or without.

It is taught, "When the pupil is ready the Master appears." And this is true, in a sense; but not as you have interpreted it.

Your secret desire for a Master will bring him to you, but only when I have prepared you for such appearance. But such appearance will be only an appearance of a Master. The true Master or Teacher, when He appears, you may never recognize; for He may be hidden in an interesting friend, a business associate, your next door neighbor, or in your own wife or husband or child. You, who have risen above Desire, you who no longer seek a Master or a Teacher, or even Me, but are abiding alone in the faith of My Eternal Presence and Promise, for you I have in store a meeting and a communion, which will bring to your Soul such joy and blessings as your human mind is incapable of conceiving.

Now, this is a mystery, and until you can comprehend it, you are justified in claiming the above as not consistent with certain statements herein, and as contradicting teachings in My other Revelations.

Fear not; this mystery will be revealed unto you if you truly wish to know My Meaning.

Until then, why, in your seeking, be satisfied with anything short of the Highest?

Why seek in human or spirit teacher, guide, master or angel, for the necessarily *limited* manifestation of My Perfection, when you can come *directly* to Me, God within you, the Omniscient, Omnipotent, Omnipresent, the Inspiring Idea back of and within *All* manifestations?

As I AM in You, even as I AM in any you seek, and as all the Wisdom, all the Power and all the Love they possess come only from *Me*, why not now come to *Me*, and let Me prepare you also so I can express My All through *You*?

You are a human personality, yet You are Divine and therefore Perfect.

The first of these truths you believe, the latter you do not believe.

Yet both are true. — That is the mystery.

You are just what you think You are.

One or the other, which are you? — Or both?

You are *One with Me*. I AM in You, in Your human personality, in Your body, mind and intellect. I AM in every cell of Your body, in every attribute of Your mind, in every faculty of Your intellect. I AM the Soul, the active Principle of each. You are in Me. You are a Cell of my Body; You are an Attribute of My Mind; You are a Faculty of My Intellect. You are a part of Me, yet You are I, My Self. We are One, and always have been.

This idea of a Master I brought to your mind's attention was only to lead you to and prepare you for this Idea of Me, your Impersonal Self, an Angel of Light, a Radiation of My Being, your own Divine Lord and Master, *within.*

Yes, *I,* your Divine Self, AM the Master your Soul has caused you to seek, and when you do find Me, and *know* I AM your Self, then will you in your human consciousness gladly become My Disciple, will lovingly wait upon Me, and will be concerned only that you faithfully serve Me, both within yourself and within your fellow men. And then will you understand why only "One is your Master, even Christ."

For I as the Christ dwell in all men and AM their One and Only Self. Through all men I AM ever calling to you and trying to reach and impress your human consciousness. As I AM continually teaching you, not only through all men but through every avenue needed at the time, I have many ways of reaching your consciousness and utilize all to bring you to a realization of My Meaning.

I speak with many voices, with the voice of all human emotions, passions and desires. I speak with Nature's voice, with the voice of Experience, even with the voice of *human* knowledge.

Yes, these are all My Voice, which I use Impersonally to express to you the one fact, that I AM in All and that I AM All. What this Voice says, in Its thousand ways, is that you, too, are part of this All, and that I AM in you, waiting for your recognition of Me and your *conscious* cooperation in the expression of Me Idea of Impersonal Perfection on earth, even as It is expressing in Heaven.

When this recognition comes, and then only, are you ready to meet and know a *real* Master. Then and then only will you realize why I, your own Impersonal Self can be and AM the only possible Master of your human personality.

Then also will you understand why in your personal, separate consciousness you could never recognize or know a real Master should you meet Him in a physical body, — that not until you are able to enter into your Christ Consciousness, My Consciousness within you and within Him, He would not exist to you other than perhaps as a kind and helpful friend or teacher.

When you have attained to that Consciousness, then only will you be worthy and qualified to know and commune with your fellows in the Great Brotherhood of the Spirit, Those who have mastered self and Who live only to help Their younger brothers also to find the Divine One within.

If a being should come into your life who seemed to you Divine and who let you think or call him a Master, he is not yet wholly Impersonal. Such a one might be a master-man, but he would not be the Divine One your Soul yearns to serve.

Perhaps you would be satisfied to have such a one for a Master, even if he were not wholly Impersonal. If so, then I would hereafter bring you to a realization of his personal imperfections by a constant comparison with My Impersonal Perfection; until you would finally turn and come to Me in complete abandon, acknowledging Me and My Impersonality as the only Model and Ideal, and as the true Cause which inspired your long search without for My Perfection, that could be found only within, hidden deep within your own Soul.

16

The Christ *and* Love

To you who fear that My Words may destroy your belief in and love for the Lord Jesus Christ, I say: Two thousand years ago, when the process of the expression of My Idea had reached the stage where I could show forth some of My Divine *Reality*, in order to do this and to recall to My human Attributes their mission on earth, it became necessary to express through a human personality and to manifest in a human form My *Divine* Attributes, so their human minds and intellects could see and remember and be inspired by Me within to let My Idea similarly express through and manifest in their human personalities.

This I did through the personality of Jesus, the man of Galilee, picturing to the human understanding by My Teachings given through Him, and by My *Life* manifested by Him, what was necessary in order to express fully My Divine Idea.

I showed, by the experiences of a symbolic nature through which I caused His human personality I created for such purpose to pass, what all personalities must pass through before you, My human Attributes, who created these personalities, can again become Impersonal enough to be conscious expressors with Me of My Divine Idea.

All of you, My human Attributes, before the I AM within can awaken your human minds to a realization of Me, your Divine Self must be born of a Virgin Love in a humble manger the place where the cattle come to feed (the humble and contrite heart filled with faith and trust in God, to which state the human or animal nature must come). You must then be taken into Egypt, the land of darkness (or intellectual activity), there to grow and thrive in body and understanding until you become strong with the feeling of Me within.

Then, when you are sufficiently conscious of *My* Power and *My* Love, will I begin to speak through you words of Wisdom and Truth, which will confound the learned of the world, even the Doctors of the Law. Then will follow a long period of study and meditation, which ripens the mind and develops the Soul, until you arrive at full maturity of the I AM Consciousness within, and which prepare you for your baptism in the Jordan, when you will be opened completely to Me, to the full consciousness that You and I are One, that there is no separation, that I AM your Real Self; and I AM henceforth permitted wholly to direct your lives.

I then *lead* you out into the world, called in My other Revelation the Wilderness, there to try you and make you strong and to accustom you to the Impersonal use of My Divine Attributes I bring to you three great Temptations of Power, Self- Righteousness, and Money, until you have proven that nothing of the intellect, nothing of the self, nothing from without, can tempt you to forget Me within, and that My Voice and Mine alone, whether speaking in your heart or in the hearts of your brothers, is the only Voice you are now capable of hearing.

This proven, there will begin the period of performing miracles and of teaching the multitude, accompanied by the revilement and persecution of the unbelieving and scoffing world; followed by the trial before Pontius Pilate, the representative of the Worldly Law; the sentence; the ascent of Calvary carrying the Cross; the being nailed upon the Cross;

the Agony; the three days in the tomb; and then the final resurrection, when you enter into complete union with Me.

All of which has its inner meaning, or Soul application, and which should be readily understood by you, if you have opened your heart to Me.

Such has been The Way in the past for you and for all who have studied and followed My Teachings, given forth in My former Revelations. Now the time has come when I have prepared you and many for a new Dispensation, wherein you can enter into the consciousness of Me direct and at once by the Impersonal Way. Those who are big enough and strong enough to throw off all claims of the human personality, and who can say I AM, and *know I AM The ONE within* Who gives them this strength and enables them to rise above the attractions and influences of the outer world, — those are the ones I have chosen through whom to express all the wondrous glories of My Divine Idea.

The Christ, or the I AM Consciousness, must be born in your heart and in the heart of every human personality, must grow and thrive and pass through in some manner every experience symbolized in the life of Jesus, before you can come to this point and become a conscious expressor with Me of My Divine Idea. The example of the Christ Love and Compassion which I expressed in that Life must you also express in some degree in your life, before you can taste of the fruits of that Love, which in reality is not love, but the Holy Three-in-One, — Love-Wisdom-Power, that is the true expression of My *Impersonal* Life.

You heretofore have not known the meaning of the Impersonal Life, hence you could not know the meaning of Impersonal Love. Love to you, if you will carefully analyze that feeling, has always been a human emotion or expression; and you have been unable to conceive of a love devoid of or unattached to some human or personal interest. Now, as you begin to feel Me within your heart and open it wide to contain Me, will I fill you with a wondrous strange new feeling, which will quicken every fiber of your being with the creative instinct, and be to you a veritable Elixir of Life. For in the outer expression of *that* feeling, when I thus, through you, pour it forth into the world, will you taste of the unutterable sweetness of My Holy Impersonal Love, with Its accompanying illumination of mind and consciousness of unlimited Power; and It will make you a wholly selfless and therefore perfect channel for the Impersonal expression of My Divine Idea.

You will then realize that you are part of Me and part of every other being, and that all you have or are, is not yours, but Mine, for Use wherever and however I direct.

Your life will no longer be centered in your self, but that self will be lost, merged in your other Selves, giving freely of your Life, your Understanding, your Strength, your Substance, which are but phases of My Impersonal Life or My Impersonal Love, that I have portioned out to you only for such use.

In the personality of Jesus, the Christ, I manifested much of the Love Impersonal, enough to inspire and lead you into seeking to emulate His Life and His Personality, and, through such seeking and striving, to awaken in you the Consciousness of the Christ within you. Through this awakening and the realization that the Christ is but the channel or door that opens unto Me, I have finally brought you to the point where you can enter in and consciously become a part of My Impersonal Life.

I here tell you plainly that My Impersonal Love has naught to do with personal lives and personal loves. All such are but the outer mediums I use through which to pour from out the heart of Humanity into the world My Real Love, where it is ever expressing its all-embracing, vitalizing, creative, and uplifting Power.

My Love considers not individuals or personalities; they are but pawns on the chessboard of life which I move as I deem best to accomplish My purpose, the full and complete expression in Humanity of My Divine Idea. In Humanity only can I express My Idea, even as you can express your idea of yourself only in and through your human personality.

In Humanity I live and move and have My Being. It is the mortal personality and body of My Immortal Self, even as your personality and its body is what you use to express your being.

All individual human personalities with their bodies are but the cells of My Body of Humanity. Just as the I AM of you is now building your body so that through it You can perfectly express My Idea of you, or your Real Self, so AM I gradually building Humanity so that through It I can perfectly express My Idea of My Self.

As the individual cells of My Body of Humanity, even as those of your human body, by partaking of My Life, become Impersonal and harmonious parts of the organs they form, they live a healthy and happy life. But let one cell oppose or act contrary to the general law of its organ, and the harmonious functioning of that organ becomes impossible, which naturally affects the whole body and results in disease.

Every cell of an organ is an integral part of that organ, and its work is necessary to that organ's perfect functioning and to the perfect health of My Body. So that unless each cell gives up all its power and all its intelligence, which are but attributes of the Life I give it, toward the perfect functioning of My entire Body, the only result for My Body can be inharmony, with its consequent effects, — disease, suffering, sin, bondage, poverty, lack of understanding, disintegration, or death.

Likewise, unless each organ gives up all the intelligence and all the powers with Which I endowed it, to the one purpose of expressing and maintaining the life of My Body in perfect health, the only result can be disorganization, disruption, rebellion, and finally WAR, — war between the various organs and between their respective cells, and a greater or lesser consequent chaotic condition in My whole Body.

In My Body of Humanity this would mean war between Nations, which are the Organs of My Body. As all war is but acute disease or disharmony, and as My Life, which in Humanity manifests as Impersonal Love, can express only in harmony — even as in the physical body, It is always utilizing, equalizing and preparing conditions so that It can thus express.

This It does either by eradicating gradually from the various organs of the body all disease, weakened and unfit cells, or by developing the disease into a malignant form in the physical body. It throws off such cells quickly by the billions, until a particular organ either is purified or its power of functioning is wholly destroyed.

In other words, the real life and work of each cell and of each organ lies in giving up its individual life that My whole Body can Be or Express in perfect harmony. When each cell and each organ has no other idea than this, and makes itself a pure and selfless channel through which My Impersonal Life can flow, then has My Body become a harmonious and perfect Whole; and then can My Idea express of earth Its Divine powers and possibilities, even as it does in the Celestial Realm of the Eternal.

As you give up your self wholly to Me that I can pour through you My Holy, Impersonal Love, having no other thought than the perfect expression of that Love, which is My Real Life, then will I through you be enabled to quicken and awaken those about you gradually to a recognition of Me, The Christ within them, so that they too will likewise give up their selves wholly to Me. Finally the organ, or that particular part of My Body of Humanity you and they form, attains perfect health and harmony, and adds its quota to the bringing about and maintaining of perfect health in My entire Body.

When such time comes, My Divine Life Force, or My Impersonal Love, will be flowing and manifesting throughout all Humanity, and My Idea will be expressing fully on earth even as It is in Heaven. The earth and all earthly bodies will no longer be of the gross physical material they formerly seemed, but they will have become utterly purified and cleansed of the self, and will have been again lifted up to whence they descended. For the purpose of their creation, that of developing organisms for the outward manifestation and human expression of My Divine Idea, will have been accomplished; and having no further use for physical or outward mediums of such expression, I hereafter will create and express only with Mind Substance, which is the only medium needed in the Heavenly World of the Impersonal Life.

17

Finding Me

You, who have studied carefully all that has been said herein, and who think you have gotten a glimpse of Me, but yet are not sure, come close, and listen with your Soul to what I now have to say.

Be still! — and KNOW, — I AM, — GOD.

If you have learned to "Be Still," if you have studied and meditated upon this "I" as God within you, if you are able to distinguish It from the personal I, and are conscious at times of being able to step outside, as it were, of your personality and view your human self as it is, see all its petty faults and weaknesses, its base selfishness, its animal appetites and passions, its childish desires and foolish pride and vanities;

If you can do all this and have seen these things with clear vision, know that at those moments you have been One with Me in consciousness, that it was your Real Self, I within you, permitting you thus to see with My Eyes the Reality of things.

At those moments you were freed from your personality and were dwelling in My Consciousness, call it Cosmic, Universal, Spiritual or Impersonal Consciousness, as you will; for you could not have seen these things in your self except through Impersonal eyes, My Eyes.

Again, if you will look back you will recall many times when you felt strongly impelled to do certain things, some of which you did, with perfect results; others of which you argued against, your intellect reasoning you into different action, and often with failure, disappointment or suffering as a result.

This impelling consciousness was only your Real Self, I within you, at such moments guiding you, distinctly telling you what to do. At those moments you were hearing with your Spiritual ears, My Ears, and when you Impersonally obeyed, success and satisfaction followed, but when you personally thought you knew better, discomfiture, regret and unhappiness resulted.

Again, there have been moments when you have *felt* approaching events, or the nearness of unseen persons, or inharmonious vibrations when contacting others.

This is only the real You feeling with your Spiritual or Impersonal Body, whose consciousness, did you but know it, is ever on the alert to protect and warn and advise you regarding all outer things, conditions and events.

The best and surest way you may know Me is when Selfless Love fills your heart, and there is a strong, compelling urge to help some one, to heal their ills, to relieve their suffering, to bring them happiness, to point out the True Way, that is the actual feel of Me within you, pushing the personality aside, using your mind and body for the purpose I created them, as avenues for the expression of My Real Nature, which is Perfect Love, the Christ of God, the one, vitalizing, quickening, life-giving, strengthening, healing, all-supplying, all-informing Power in the Universe.

All this is pointed out to you in order to impress upon you that it is I, in your Spiritual body, the Perfect Body within, where I dwell, Who AM always thus talking to you, advising you, teaching you, warning and helping you, in all the affairs of life, yes, in every little detail.

If you will but turn to Me, and will carefully watch for and study these impressions which you are receiving every moment, and will learn to trust them, and thus to wait upon and rest in Me, putting all your faith in Me, verily I will guide you in all your ways; I will solve for you all your problems, make easy all your work, and you will be led among green pastures, beside the still waters of life.

Ah, My child, if you will spend but one-tenth of the time and energy you have wasted in seeking without among the husks of human knowledge and human teachings, in earnest, determined efforts directed within to find Me;

If you will devote but one hour each day thus to Me alone, imagining and practicing the Presence of Me within you;

I here promise you that you will not only soon, very soon find Me, but I will be to you an exhaustless fount of such Wisdom and Strength and Help, as your human mind now cannot possibly conceive.

Yes, if you will but seek Me thus, making Me FIRST in your life, never resting until you do find Me, it will not be long before you will become conscious of My Presence, of My Loving Voice, speaking constantly from out of the depths of your heart.

You will learn to come to Me in Sweet Communion, and you will find yourself abiding in My consciousness, and that My Word is abiding in you, and that whatever you desire will in seemingly miraculous ways be done unto you.

This abiding *continually* in Me may be difficult at first, for the World, the Flesh and the Devil are still presenting evidence to your consciousness. But you will become accustomed to the use of My Impersonal Eyes, and will soon be able to see into the Reality of things, even into the Reality of these seeming Lords of the Earth. Then you will find you are dwelling in a wondrous new World, peopled with Angelic Beings, using the Flesh bodies of Their human personalities merely as vehicles, or instruments, or clothing, in which to contact the earthly conditions and experiences They have created, in order to develop the Soul qualities necessary for the perfect expression on earth of *My Idea.*

To your eyes then there will be no shadows, no evil, and consequently no Devil; for all is Light and Love, Freedom, Happiness and Peace, and you will see *Me in all*, in each Being some attribute of Me, in each animate thing some phase of Me; and you will need only to let My Love shine from out your heart and It will illumine for you the Real meaning of *all* that you see.

Then the great Realization will come that you have found the Kingdom of God, that you are walking in It, that It is right here on this earth, that It is manifesting all around you, that you have been living in It all the time, but you did not know it;

That instead of being without in some far off place, It is within your own being, within every other being, the innermost inner of all manifested things.

In other words, It will be found to be the REALITY of ALL things, and that all outward seeming is but the shadow of this Reality, created by man's misconceptions and his belief in his separateness from Me.

When you have found The Kingdom, you will likewise find your place in It, realizing now that you are in truth one of My Divine Attributes, that your work was all laid out for you from the beginning, and that all that has gone before has been but a preparation and a fitting of your human personality for that work.

Your whole Soul will leap with joyful anticipation, that, after all these many years of wandering, you have at last returned to My Home, and can now enter into My Real Life, One in Consciousness with Me and with your other Selves, all working to bring about the final perfect expression on earth of My Divine Idea.

You, to whom the reading of this has brought memories of previous joys and whose Soul has quickened in response, do not leave these words until you have gotten from them all I have to tell you.

Be Still! And listen to My inner Voice, and learn of the glories that await if you are able to see with Impersonal Eyes and hear with Impersonal Understanding.

However, if this reading brings to you your first vision of My Reality within you, setting in motion, by this partial realization of Me and My Kingdom, high vibrations which lift you into a temporary Spiritual ecstasy, and you resolve to try to abide always in this Consciousness of Me, and always to obey Me, do not be discouraged should you fail when immediately thereafter an occasion comes to test the sincerity and strength of your resolve.

It is only by your trying and failing and realizing keenly your lack of strength and ability to rest and trust in Me, that I can quicken in you the consciousness of My Divine Powers ever waiting to manifest through you.

These high vibrations are only the arousing into action of certain *Soul* qualities and their corresponding faculties, which must be awakened before I can manifest such Powers.

And naturally when such Soul qualities are aroused, they meet active opposition from certain other qualities which heretofore held undisputed sway in your nature, and which must be overcome and brought under subjection and then lifted up into their true service before the Soul qualities can freely express.

And this opposition should and will strengthen and test and perfect the expression of these Soul qualities, for you must be capable of withstanding every attack from without before you can fully manifest all My Divine Powers pushing forth from within.

Know that I AM manifesting these Powers in you just as fast as you can bear it and be strong. The mistake you make is in trying to grow yourself.

I AM the Tree of Life within you. My Life will and must push forth, but It will do it by gradual and steady growth. You cannot come into your fruitage before you have grown to it. Remember, My Life is all the time building you up into the perfection of health and strength and beauty, that must express outwardly as It is even now expressing within.

You who have begun to realize I AM within, but have not yet learned to commune with Me, listen and learn now.

You have learned to "Be Still," and you have perhaps *felt* My Presence within. If so, realizing I AM there, ask Me a question. Then, with a silent, earnest prayer to Me for an answer, but without anxiety, care or personal interest, and with an open mind, wait confidently for the impressions that will come.

Should a thought come in answer that you recognize as what you have heard or read somewhere, cast it out immediately, and say, "No. Father, what do you say?"

Other thoughts may come from other human sources, but if you are alert you will recognize them as such and refuse to accept them. Then if you *persist* in asking *Me, you* will finally get an answer that you will *feel* is really from Me.

Thus it will be at *first*. When you have learned to distinguish My Voice from all other voices, and can keep your personal interest wholly suppressed, then will you be able to hold silent communion with Me at will, without interference from others' ideas, beliefs, and opinions; and you can ask any question you wish, or another can ask you any question on any problem on which they need help, and *I will that moment place in your mind the words to speak,* either silently to yourself, or audibly through your tongue to the other.

You, My Beloved, who have consecrated your self to Me, and are bending every effort to find union with Me, but instead have found apparently that every prop of the World's support has been withdrawn or is being withdrawn, and that you are without money and without friends and know not where to turn for human help;

Learn, My Blessed One, that you are very, very close now, and that if you will only continue to abide in Me, letting My Word abide in and guide you, resting and trusting absolutely in My Promise, I will very soon bring to you a Joy, a Fulfillment, a Peace, that human words and human minds cannot possibly picture.

For you have obeyed My Commands, and you have trusted Me, and have sought first My Kingdom and My Righteousness, and therefore will I add all other things unto you, even those the World has denied you.

You, My Dear One, who likewise have consecrated your self to Me, but who are still holding to some of the World's standards, being unable to let go and trust wholly to Me;

You to whom, therefore, I have permitted failure, disappointment, even poverty, in order to let you learn the false value of all worldly things, their impermanence, their lack of power to provide happiness, their having nothing to do with My Real Life;

You, dear child, who do not yet see this and whose heart is full of anxiety and fear because you do not see where tomorrow's bread is coming from, or the money for next week's rent, or for the past due mortgage;

Listen once more to My Words long since given to you in the Sermon on the Mount.

"Therefore I say unto you, Take no thought for your life, what ye shall eat or what ye shall drink; nor yet for your body, what ye shall put on. Is not the life more than meat, and the body than raiment?"

"Behold the fowls of the air; for they sow not, neither do they reap, nor gather into barns; yet your heavenly Father feedeth them. Are ye not much better than they?"

"Which of you by taking thought can add one cubit unto his stature?"

"And why take ye thought for raiment? Consider the lilies of the field, how they grow; they toil not neither do they spin; and yet I say unto you that even Solomon in all his glory was not arrayed like one of these."

"Wherefore, if God so clothe the grass of the field, which today is and tomorrow is cast into the oven, shall he not much more clothe you, O ye of little faith?"

"Therefore take no thought, saying, What shall we eat? Or What shall we drink? Or wherewithal shall we be clothed?"

"For your heavenly Father knoweth that ye have need of these things."

"But seek ye first the kingdom of God (being interpreted His Consciousness) and His righteousness; and all these things shall be added unto you."

"Take, therefore, no thought for the morrow, for the morrow shall take thought for the things of itself."

"Sufficient unto the day is the evil thereof."

Do you need any more definite Commands or any more definite Promise than these? — You who have consecrated yourself to Me, and call yourself My disciple. Listen!

Have I not always provided everything? Have you ever been in need but what I always appeared with help just at the right moment? Has there ever been a time when things looked dark that I did not bring Light?

Can you, with what you know now, look back over your life and see where you could have ordered it better? Would you exchange your *Spiritual* understanding for the earthly possessions of any one you know? Have I not done all this, despite the fact you have been rebelling and refusing to listen to Me all your life?

Ah, My Children, can you not see that money, home, clothes, food, and their acquirement are only incidents and have nothing to do with your real Life, excepting as you make them real by thinking into them so much importance, and letting Me remain only a side issue?

If it becomes necessary for you to be deprived of the things of the world that you may learn the Truth, — that I AM the *only* important thing in Life, that I must be FIRST if you *truly* love Me, — I permit this that real and lasting Happiness and Prosperity can be yours.

This applies to you also, My Child, you who have lost health, have lost courage, have lost all hold of your Self, and after weary years of seeking without from earthly physicians and remedies, following faithfully every instruction and suggestion given, in order to regain the Life you have lost, — you who have turned finally within to Me, with the faint hope that I may be able to help you.

Know, My Little One, that you, too, must come in complete surrender to Me, the One and Only Physician who can heal you. For I AM the Life Omnipotent within you. I AM your Health, your Strength, your Vitality. Not until you can feel *ME* within, and know I AM all this to you, is real and lasting Health for you to experience.

And now, My Child, draw close. For I AM now going to tell you the means of obtaining all these things — Health, Prosperity, Happiness, Union, Peace.

In the following words lies hidden the Great Secret. Blessed be you who find it.

Be still! And KNOW, — I AM, — GOD.

KNOW I AM *in you.* KNOW I AM *you.* KNOW I AM your LIFE. KNOW *All* Wisdom, *All* Love, *All* Power abides in this Life, which is flowing freely through your entire being *NOW.*

I *AM* the LIFE, I *AM* the INTELLIGENCE, I *AM* the POWER in *all* Substance, — in all the cells of your body; in the cells of all mineral, vegetable and animal matter; in fire, water and air; in Sun, Moon and Stars. I AM that in you and in them which IS. Their consciousness is One with your consciousness, and All is My Consciousness. Through My Consciousness in them All that they have or are is yours — for the asking.

Speak in the Consciousness of your Oneness with Me.

Speak in the Consciousness of My Power in you and of My Intelligence in them.

Speak — COMMAND what You WILL in this Consciousness, — and the Universe will rush to obey.

RISE UP! O aspirant for union with Me. Accept now your Divine Heritage! Open wide your Soul, your mind, your body, and breathe in My Breath of Life!

KNOW that I AM filling you full to overflowing with My Divine POWER, that every fiber, every nerve, every cell, every atom of your being is now *consciously ALIVE* with Me, alive with My Health, with My Strength, with Intelligence with *My BE-ING!*

For I AM *within* you. We are not separated. We could not possibly be separated. For I AM *You.* I AM your *REAL* Self, your *REAL* Life and I AM manifesting My SELF and *ALL MY POWERS* in you *NOW.*

AWAKE! Rise up and assert your Sovereignty! *KNOW* your *SELF* and your POWERS! KNOW that *all I have is yours*, that My Omnipotent LIFE is flowing through you, that you can take of IT and build with IT what you WILL, and IT will manifest for you as Health, Power, Prosperity, Union, Happiness, Peace,— anything you WILL of ME.

Imagine this. THINK it. KNOW it! Then, with all the *Positiveness* of your nature, *Speak the Creative WORD!* It will not return to you void.

But know, Beloved, that this cannot be until you have come to Me in complete and utter surrender, until you have given yourself, your substance, your affairs, your Life into My keeping, putting all care and responsibility upon Me, resting and trusting in Me absolutely.

When you have done this, then will the above Words quicken into active life My Divine Powers latent in your Soul, and you will be conscious of a Mighty FORCE within you, which, just to the extent that you abide in Me, and let My Words abide in you, will free you entirely from your Dream World, will quicken you fully in Spirit, will make all the way clear for you, supply all things you desire, and lift trouble and suffering from you forevermore. Then will there be no more doubts and questionings, for you will KNOW that I, God your very Self, will always provide, will always point out the way; for You will have found that *You and I are One.*

18

Union

Y ou, who truly wish to consecrate yourself thus to Me, and are willing to give your whole Life to Me, putting aside all personal ideas, hopes and aims, in order that I may freely and fully express through you My Impersonal Idea, listen carefully to these Words.

I have led you through all your experiences of life up to just this point. If you are now really ready and willing to serve Me, and have learned that you, of yourself, can know nothing and can do nothing, and that I AM, and what you call *your* intelligence and *your* strength and *your* substance are really Mine, and that it is I who direct all your thoughts and both cause and enable you to do all that you do, — then can you comprehend the significance of My Words, and are quite prepared to obey them.

I have hitherto brought to you the experiences that would teach you just these things. But now, if you are ready and worthy, you shall work *consciously* with Me, joyfully yet calmly awaiting each new experience, knowing that in each are contained marvelous expressions of My Meaning, which I will make altogether clear to you, and which will more and more bring you into loving, intimate union with *Me*.

Thus all experiences will hereafter be blessings, instead of trials and tests, or karmic effects of previous acts; for in each will I disclose unto you glorious visions of My Reality — of your own True, Wonderful Self; until you no longer will have any disposition to follow any of the old desires but will seek only to know My wishes and to please Me.

This will manifest in many new ways. In your activities, be they what they may, you will care not what the task, but do whatever lies before you, knowing that is what I require; and striving always and only to please Me by your *Impersonal* part in the doing, which enables Me thus speedily to accomplish My Will.

In your business even, you will find I AM there. In fact, it is I Who provide you with such business, whatever it be; not that in it you can be the success or the failure or the common plodder you are, nor that you can pile up riches for your descendants, or lose all that you have, or never accumulate any. No, but that through the success or failure, or lack of ambition or special ability, I may quicken your heart to a realization of Me, The Impersonal One, seated within; inspiring and directing all these things that you do, waiting for you consciously to participate in the *true* Success and accept of the *real* Riches I have in store for you.

You will then learn that your business, or labor, or condition of life, are but incidents, or the outer vehicles I choose and use to carry you through certain experiences which I deem best adapted to bring you to this realization; and at the same time to quicken in you certain Soul qualities that now but imperfectly express.

If you can but *know* Me, dwelling thus in your heart, accompanying you to your office, to your shop, to your labor, whatever it be, and will permit Me to direct your business and all your ways; verily I say unto you, when you can do this, you will at once become conscious of a new Power within you, a Power that will flow forth from you as a gentle, kindly sympathy, a true brotherliness, a loving helpfulness to all with whom you come in contact, inspiring them to higher principles of business and of life, creating in them a longing to shed a similar influence within their own circle; a Power that will attract to you business, money, friends, and abundance of all things you need; a Power that will connect you with the highest realms of thought, enabling you both to vision clearly and to manifest consciously all My Impersonal Powers and Attributes every moment of your life.

You will no longer feel any need to go to church or to religious meetings of any kind, or even to read the teachings of My Revelations, in order to find Me and to worship Me.

Instead you will turn *within* and always find Me *there*, and you will be so filled with the joy of communing with and serving Me, and of thus worshipping Me, that you will care not for any other thing than just to listen to and obey My Voice, and to feel the warmth and thrill of My Tender Love, as It fills and surrounds you and prepares the way and softens the conditions wherever you go and whatever be your work.

You I will cause to be an uplifting and leavening influence in the community wherever I send you, drawing all men to Me to receive My Blessing through you, who now are able so to make your personality subservient to My Holy Impersonality that they forget you and see only Me, and feel the quickening of My Presence within their own hearts; so that they go forth with a new light in their eyes and the sense of a new purpose in *their* lives.

In your homes particularly will I dwell, Through those nearest you, will I teach you many wonderful things, which now you can understand, when before you passionately rebelled against their truth. Through husband, wife, child, brother, sister, parent, will I now be able to develop in you these great qualities, patience, gentleness, forbearance, tongue-control, loving-kindness, true unselfishness, and an understanding heart; for I will cause you to see that I AM deep down in their hearts as I AM in yours.

Now will you be able to appreciate this and profit by it. When you truly do comprehend this great truth you will be able to see *Me* in your brother or your wife or your parent or child, appealing to you with loving, joyful eyes, when they speak. Instead of blaming them for their seeming mistakes, you will turn within to Me, the Impersonal One, Who will speak through you gentle words of loving kindness, which will immediately soften the heart of the other, and bring you once more together, and closer than ever before. For I, the real I, in the heart of each, AM One, *and always respond when thus called upon.*

Yes, if you can but know it, your greatest school and your greatest teacher is in your own home, by your own fireside. Much, very much is reserved for those who consciously know this and permit Me, the Impersonal One within, to do the teaching. For I will not only teach you many things through the mouths of those nearest you, but I will teach those others similarly through you, but with this difference: if you are conscious of Me and Impersonally are resting in Me and My Wisdom, then you will permit Me to inspire your words and to empower your acts, and you will not be concerned about their effects upon others or upon yourself, putting all responsibility upon Me.

When you can do this, you will marvel at the changes you see taking place, both in your personality and in the personalities of your dear ones — until you are able to see, back of their human personalities, Me, your own Impersonal Self, shining from out their eyes.

When you *can* thus see Me, then will the heavens be opened unto you, and no more will you see flaws in you brother, or hear inharmony around you, or feel unkindness coming from any other fellow being. For you will *know* that I, the Impersonal One, within that other, AM the fount of all perfection, of all harmony, of all loving-kindness, and wait but for the human personality to make the recognition, step submissively aside, and let My Light shine forth, resplendent in all the glory of My Divine Idea.

Then will you see that all conditions in which I put you are the places I have chosen where you can best serve Me; that in all places and in all conditions there is much, very much to do. The more objectionable they are to the personality, the more need there is of My Living Presence.

Wherever you are when the awakening comes, whatever has been your training, — in business, in a profession, in manual labor, in the church, or in the underworld, — there lies perhaps your best opportunity to serve; for there you know best the manner and the way. For how can My and Your other selves awaken to a knowledge of My Presence within, without the quickening influence which must first come from without.

You who have received must give. You who have been quickened must become the quickener. You must take into this business, into this profession, into this labor, into this underworld, My Living Presence, must open the doors of the saddened and sickened heart and let My Light and My Healing Love pour in. You must supply the leaven that will leaven the lump. If these conditions are to be lifted up, you, My awakened one, must carry to these, My ignorant and betrayed ones, My Inspiration, My Blessing, My Strength, that they can rise up and throw off the influence of the world's ways, can harken to My Voice within, and can hereafter be the master of surrounding conditions and no longer the slave. No condition in life can be lifted up or conquered by running away from it. The Divine touch is needed and must be supplied. It can only be supplied by one who has sounded the depths as well as reached the heights of human experience, with *Me* as Guide and Interpreter.

You who read, and whose Soul comprehends, are blessed, and your work lies before you.

But you who still hesitate while your personality quakes in fear as the Light filters through your clouded intellect, — you, too, will soon partake of My Blessings; for I AM rapidly preparing you for the joy that awaits.

Both you who comprehend and you who fear, know that I AM even now manifesting My Will through you; and the time will surely come when you will know no other Will but Mine, and when all things You Will, will come to pass and you will awaken fully from your Dream of Separation, and know Me as your Real and Only Self.

This will not be until you have given yourself and everything in your life wholly over to Me, and there is nothing left in *your* human personality to attract from others the slightest inharmonious thought or feeling, by act or word of yours.

Your way *then* will be one continuous round of blessing. Wherever you go will My Light shine and My Love radiate forth about you, creating Peace, Concord, Unity. The great thing will be, though not great but natural when once you understand, that every one will be better and happier by reason of your appearance in their lives.

For the I AM in them, while still in the flesh, has found or sensed within you a truly Impersonal avenue of expression, and therefore feels, though not consciously by the personality, the Glory and the Holiness of My Impersonal Life.

Prayer[2]

Beloved Father; Thou Oh blessed Christ Jesus; and Thou our dear Brothers and Sisters of the Kingdom... hear this, our earnest prayer.

Draw us in consciousness deep within where Thou art, where self exists not and where we may be one with Thee and abide with Thee in Christ.

Help us to open wide our hearts and let out Thy Great Love that It may possess us utterly, rule, motivate and inspire our every thought, word and act, merging us completely with Love, thereby enabling us to love as Thou Lovest, to see as Thou seest, to hear as Thou hearest; lifting the consciousness of our human minds into complete oneness with our Christ Consciousness – Thy Consciousness; so that henceforth we may consciously, at will, be with Thee, work with Thee, commune with Thee, face to face, at all times and on all planes, when the need is in the Father's Service; and we may know with Thy Understanding all things we seek and need to know.

Cleanse us of all consciousness of Self and separation from Thee, so that our Lord Christ henceforth may live His Life in us, do His Will in us, be His Self in us, without let or hindrance of any kind, for evermore.

---

[2] From *The Way to the Kingdom-*

Beloved Father, make us to abide always in Thy Consciousness and Thy Word to abide in us, giving us ever of Thy Wisdom to light and direct our way, Thy Will to strengthen and sustain us and Thy Love to surround, protect and fill us; so that we may see Thee, dear Christ, may feel thy glorious presence within us, may know Thee, may be truly One with Thee, everywhere, in everything, and in every one of our brothers and sisters.

We thank and glorify Thee, beloved Father, for Thy many Blessings. Take us wholly unto Thyself, so that we may be selfless and perfect instruments for Thy use.

In Christ Jesus' Name we ask it. Amen

Joseph S Benner

(1872–1941)

CPSIA information can be obtained at www.ICGtesting.com
Printed in the USA
LVOW07s1019160615

442659LV00002B/110/P

9 781603 866712